German Romantic Partsongs

Deutsches Chorbuch der Romantik

Selected, edited, and translated by
Herausgegeben von

JUDITH BLEZZARD

Music Department
OXFORD UNIVERSITY PRESS
Oxford and New York

Oxford University Press, Walton Street, Oxford OX2 6DP, England
Oxford University Press, 200 Madison Avenue, New York, NY 10016, USA

Music origination by Barnes Music Engraving Ltd., East Sussex
Printed in Great Britain by J. W. Arrowsmith Ltd., Bristol

Contents

Introduction

This collection of partsongs, all for unaccompanied SATB, reflects the development of German music for small mixed choral forces from the early nineteenth century until the early twentieth, a period in which it was marked by increasing resourcefulness, expressiveness, and diversity. Like other musical forms with which it developed concurrently to a certain extent, such as German opera and the solo song with piano accompaniment, the partsong flourished largely as a manifestation of the upsurge in German national consciousness combined with the growing awareness of individual sensibilities that was a characteristic of early Romanticism. Renewed interest in older choral music and in folksong also contributed. But the main impetus for the unprecedented flowering of the partsong in Germany as the nineteenth century progressed was twofold: the establishment of choirs to sing the music, together with the development of a rich repertory of German Romantic poetry that provided the inspiration for the composers represented here.

In retrospect, the most significant event relating to the inception of new choirs in Germany was the formation of a music society known as the *Liedertafel* in Berlin in 1809 by Mendelssohn's teacher Carl Friedrich Zelter. Monthly meetings of the *Liedertafel* were held at which new compositions were sung by its members. For his time, Zelter's views on music education and the propagation of new music were innovatory, and the *Liedertafel* provided the model for several similar organizations throughout Germany.

As in England a little earlier with the establishment of glee clubs, the aim of the choirs that sprang up in Germany in the early nineteenth century was just as much convivial as it was musical. Consequently the need arose for music that could be sung by amateur musicians without too much difficulty in congenial rather than formal or large-scale surroundings. At first these German choirs, like their English counterparts, were exclusively male. In Germany the tradition of the men's choir, often linked by perpetuation of local customs and traditional costume to specifically rural activities such as hunting and harvest, still persists, with its own repertory of music which is completely distinct from that for mixed choir. Indeed, some composers, such as Marschner, Weber, and even Wagner, produced their entire output of partsongs for TTBB only. As the nineteenth century progressed, mixed choirs began to proliferate in both England and Germany: a further parallel between the two countries' development of choral music was the establishment of choral festivals which provided a further stimulus for the composition of music for choirs. As well as unaccompanied choral music, there are notable examples of music for small choir with piano accompaniment from this period. Most of Schubert's mixed partsongs have piano accompaniment, and the best-known examples are possibly the two sets of *Liebeslieder* waltzes by Brahms.

The poets whose work appears set to music in this collection are as varied in talent and literary stature as their poems are in subject-matter. The collection contains several settings of texts by Johann Wolfgang von Goethe, while German folksong and an unabashed love-poem in Plattdeutsch (a Low German dialect from the north of the country with its own literature and without implications of social class) occur alongside the finely-wrought Romantic effusions of poets such as Friedrich Rückert, Heinrich Heine, and Paul Heyse, whose works are better known as the texts of some of the most significant accompanied solo songs and song-cycles of the nineteenth century. A few of the poets in the collection are virtually unknown, and owe the survival of their works to the choice of texts by a composer of more significant talent than their own. Many of the poems are about love, often lost or unrequited; others are concerned with nature, the seasons, hunting, life and death, religion and folklore, or the expression of a human ideal or moral point.

Schubert's contribution to the unaccompanied partsong repertory is small, exceeded in size and variety by those of Loewe and Spohr, both of whose partsongs are often characterised by chromaticism and florid writing for dramatic effect, even in some of the shorter pieces. Some of Mendelssohn's output of partsongs was designed deliberately to be sung out of doors for the singers' recreation: even so, they make delightful informal concert pieces. On his visits to England, Mendelssohn may well have been influenced by the English glee and partsong. A reciprocal influence is present as well: from the more meditative Mendelssohn pieces in particular it is easy to recognise the extent to which, in both style and sentiment, they were to inform (and even to supply material for) the later Victorian partsong, anthem, and hymn.

Schumann's large-scale choral works are sometimes regarded as stilted and uninspired, yet the smaller choral pieces show many of the best features of his solo songs and chamber music in their lyricism and sense of inner propulsion. His sensitivity towards the words is clear: in the atmospherically vivid *Der Schmidt*, for example, he achieves effect by exploiting the sounds of the words as well as reflecting on the meaning of the text as a whole. The partsongs of both Robert Franz and Niels Gade (a Dane working in Leipzig) are of a consistently high quality. Those of Franz have more in common with Schubert and are less overtly passionate than many of Schumann's, while Gade's gain some of their appeal from his colourful use of vocal textures.

The first six pieces in the Cornelius group all date from around 1842 when the seventeen-year-old Cornelius was already earning his living as violinist, actor, and composer. These previously unpublished pieces appear in manuscript as extensively altered sketches, but their occasional lack of technical expertise is more than compensated for by their originality and spontaneity of expression. The strategic use of modulation and grouping of forces in different registers is reminiscent of Schubert—but the Schubert of chamber music and solo song rather than of the partsong. The final item in the Cornelius set, his last musical composition, is more accomplished but still retains the warmth and vigour of his early partsongs.

Bruckner's partsongs, essentially small in scale, show occasional glimpses of the transcendental quality, grandeur and poise that typify his church music. His sketch for the previously unpublished *Du bist wie eine Blume*, with its repeated attempts at a diffuse middle section, shows Bruckner grappling to contain the proportions of this delicately-wrought piece whilst at the same time allowing his inspiration its due measure of freedom. Of all the composers represented in this collection, Brahms is clearly the most significant and original in the field of the partsong and, indeed, of choral music in general. In addition to his knowledge of the partsongs of Mendelssohn and Schumann in particular, Brahms maintained a lifelong interest in folksong and in early polyphony. Like most of his partsongs, the six pieces in the present collection all betray one or more of these diverse influences: the last of them to be composed, a setting of Klaus Groth's poem *Im Herbst*, shows how, as in much of his unaccompanied church music, Brahms fuses tightly-woven partwriting with an expansive approach to overall form, harmony and development of material.

The partsongs in this collection by Wolf and Schoenberg all date from their composers' early years. As the nineteenth century drew to a close, there was an increasing tendency for unaccompanied choral music (both sacred and secular) to be directed towards use by more highly accomplished choirs. Wolf's set of *Sechs geistliche Lieder* (1881) on texts by Eichendorff illustrates this trend; Schoenberg's *Friede auf Erden* (1907) epitomises it. By contrast, the three pieces by the seventeen-year-old Wolf present no problems; clearly conceived for small-scale amateur performance, they are firmly rooted in the Romantic tradition. Schoenberg's exuberant Plattdeutsch setting dates from the period in his early twenties when he was associated with various choral societies in Vienna.

Later in the twentieth century the German partsong tradition has been maintained and its boundaries widened by the work of composers such as Paul Hindemith, Anton Webern, Hans Pfitzner, Richard Strauss, Ernst Pepping, and Hugo Distler. But this diversification tended to submerge the impetus and spontaneity of the early nineteenth-century concept of the partsong and it is this, together with its refreshing romantic idealism, which encapsulates the appeal of these nineteenth-century German partsongs today for singers and listeners alike.

I should like to acknowledge with gratitude the help of the following institutions and individuals. The staff of the British Library, London, and the Österreichische Nationalbibliothek, Vienna enabled me to gain access to otherwise unobtainable music by Cornelius, Franz, Gade, Loewe, and Spohr. The authorities at Liverpool University kindly awarded me a small grant to assist with the initial costs of obtaining material for this project. I owe a debt of gratitude also to Dr Robert Danbury, Miss Elizabeth Danbury, and Mr Bill Fox for help on German grammatical issues; to Herr Professor Gotthilf Ehninger and Frau Renate Beck-Ehninger for providing background material and for details of textual layout; to Mr Otto and Mrs Gerda Horwich for their readings and prose translations of the Cornelius manuscript texts, and for their generous help with my own translations of the remaining texts, and to Mr Michael Rigelsford for his prose translation of the Plattdeutsch text by Klaus Groth set to music by Schoenberg. I am indebted most of all to my family for their patience and good-humoured help as my work has progressed, to all the singers with whom I have much enjoyed working on this and other repertories, and to James Denny (1908–78), Professor of Music at Leeds University, who so perceptively fostered my early interest in music for chamber choir, and to whose memory this edition is dedicated.

JUDITH BLEZZARD
October 1989

Vorwort

Diese Sammlung von mehrstimmigen Liedern, alle für gemischten Chor ohne Begleitung, spiegelt die Entwicklung der deutschen Musik für kleinere gemischte Chöre vom frühen 19. bis zum frühen 20. Jahrhundert wider, also einer Zeit, in der diese Musik an Einfallsreichtum, Ausdruckskraft und Vielfalt gewann. Wie die anderen Musikformen, die sich ungefähr zur gleichen Zeit entwickelten, zum Beispiel die deutsche Oper und das Lied mit Klavierbegleitung, erlebte das mehrstimmige Lied seine Blüte vor allem als Ausdruck des wachsenden deutschen Nationalgefühls in Verbindung mit dem zunehmenden Bewußtsein für die Empfindungen des Einzelnen, das für die frühe Romantik kennzeichnend war. Auch das wiederauflebende Interesse an älterer Chormusik und Volksmusik trug dazu bei. Aber die beiden wichtigsten Gründe für diese beispiellose Blüte des mehrstimmigen Liedes in Deutschland im Laufe des 19. Jahrhunderts waren zum einen die Entstehung von Chören, die diese Lieder singen konnten, und zum anderen die Entwicklung einer reichhaltigen Auswahl an deutscher romantischer Dichtung, von der sich die hier vertretenen Komponisten inspirieren ließen.

Zurückblickend läßt sich sagen, daß das wichtigste Ereignis, das die Entstehung neuer Chöre in Deutschland beeinflußte, die Gründung eines Musikvereins, *Die Liedertafel*, durch Mendelssohns Lehrer Carl Friedrich Zelter im Jahre 1809 in Berlin war. Die Mitglieder der *Liedertafel* trafen sich jeden Monat, um neue Kompositionen zu singen. Für die damalige Zeit hatte Zelter sehr moderne Ansichten über Musikerziehung und die Verbreitung von neuer Musik, und die *Liedertafel* wurde zum Modell für mehrere ähnliche Vereine in ganz Deutschland.

Diese im frühen 19. Jahrhundert in Deutschland gebildeten Chöre dienten nicht nur der Musik, sondern auch der Geselligkeit, ähnlich wie die etwas eher in England entstandenen *glee clubs*. (*Glees* waren einfache mehrstimmige englische Lieder ohne Begleitung, anfangs nur für Männerstimmen, die oft von Themen wie Essen und Trinken handelten, bis das Genre später verfeinert wurde.) So entstand ein Bedarf nach Liedern, die von Laienmusikern ohne größere Schwierigkeiten in einer geselligen Atmosphäre im kleinen Rahmen gesungen werden konnten. Zunächst waren diese deutschen Chöre, ebenso wie ihre Gegenstücke in England, reine Männerchöre. In Deutschland besteht die Tradition des Männerchors auch heute noch; Männerchöre sind oft durch den Fortbestand regionaler Bräuche und Trachten eng mit dem Landleben, z.B. der Jagd oder der Ernte, verbunden und haben ihr eigenes Musikrepertoire, das mit dem Repertoire von gemischten Chören keinerlei Ähnlichkeit aufweist. Einige Komponisten wie beispielsweise Marschner, Weber und sogar Wagner, schrieben alle ihre mehrstimmigen Lieder nur für Männerchöre. Im Laufe des 19. Jahrhunderts entstanden aber sowohl in England als auch in Deutschland mehr und mehr gemischte Chöre. Eine weitere Parallele in der Entwicklung der Chormusik in den beiden Ländern bestand in der Begründung von Chorfestspielen, die wiederum einen Anlaß für die Komposition von Chormusik boten. Aus dieser Zeit gibt es nicht nur unbegleitete Chormusik, sondern auch bedeutende Beispiele für Stücke für kleinere Chöre mit Klavierbegleitung. Schuberts Lieder für gemischten Chor haben zumeist eine Klavierbegleitung, und die bekanntesten Beispiele sind wohl Brahms' Walzer *Liebeslieder*.

Die Dichter, deren Werke in dieser Sammlung vertont sind, unterscheiden sich in ihrem Talent und ihrer literarischen Bedeutung so sehr wie ihre Gedichte in ihren Themen. Die Sammlung enthält mehrere Vertonungen von Texten von Johann Wolfgang von Goethe, aber auch deutsche Volkslieder und ein unverfrorenes plattdeutsches Liebeslied, und daneben die sorgfältig ausgearbeiteten romantischen Ergüsse von Dichtern wie Friedrich Rückert, Heinrich Heine, und Paul Heyse, dessen Werke vor allem als die Texte der bedeutendsten Solo-Lieder und Liederzyklen mit Begleitung des 19. Jahrhunderts bekannt sind. Einige der in dieser Sammlung vertretenen Dichter sind so gut wie unbekannt und verdanken das Überdauern ihrer Werke nur der Tatsache, daß ein ihnen an Talent überlegener Komponist sie als Liedertext auswählte. Viele dieser Gedichte handeln von Liebe, oft hoffnungslos oder unerwidert, andere befassen sich mit der Natur, den Jahreszeiten, der Jagd, mit Leben und Tod, Religion und Folklore, oder sie beschreiben ein menschliches Ideal oder eine moralische Lehre.

Schuberts Beitrag zum unbegleiteten mehrstimmigen Lied ist recht klein, Loewes und Spohrs dagegen größer und vielseitiger. Die mehrstimmigen Lieder der beiden letzteren Komponisten, selbst einige der kürzeren Werke, sind oft durch Chromatik und einen blumigen Stil zur Erzielung dramatischer Effekte gekennzeichnet. Einige von Mendelssohns Liedern für gemischten Chor wurden ausdrücklich für den Vortrag im Freien zur Erbauung der Sänger komponiert, sie eignen sich aber ebensogut als wunderschöne informelle Konzertstücke. Bei seinen Englandbesuchen ist Mendelssohn wahrscheinlich vom englischen *glee* und mehrstimmigen Lied beeinflußt worden. Der Einfluß ist auch in die andere Richtung zu spüren: Vor allem an den meditativeren Mendelssohn-Stücken kann man gut erkennen, in welchem Maße sie sowohl stilistisch als auch gefühlsmäßig die späteren viktorianischen mehrstimmigen Lieder und Hymnen beeinflussen und sogar Material dafür liefern sollten.

Schumanns größere Chorwerke gelten manchmal als gestelzt und wenig inspiriert, doch seine kleineren Chorstücke enthalten viele der besten Eigenschaften seiner Solo-Lieder und Kammermusik, besonders in ihrer Gefühlsbetontheit und inneren Antriebskraft. Sein Gespür für den Text ist deutlich: Im atmosphärischen *Der Schmidt* beispielsweise nutzt er sowohl den Klang der einzelnen Wörter als auch den Text als Ganzes wirkungsvoll aus. Die mehrstimmigen Lieder von Robert Franz und Niels Gade (ein Däne, der in Leipzig arbeitete) sind von durchgehend guter Qualität. Franz' Werke haben mehr mit Schubert gemeinsam und sind nicht so leidenschaftlich wie viele Lieder Schumanns, wohingegen Gades Stücke durch seine lebhafte Verwendung der unterschiedlichen Stimmen besonders ansprechend wirken.

Die ersten sechs Stücke in der Cornelius-Gruppe stammen alle aus der Zeit um 1842, als der siebzehnjährige Cornelius schon seinen Lebensunterhalt als Geiger, Schauspieler und Komponist verdiente. Diese bisher unveröffentlichten Stücke sind in den Originalhandschriften als vielfach geänderte Entwürfe zu erkennen, aber ihr gelegentlicher Mangel an technischem Schliff wird durch ihre Originalität und Spontaneität mehr als ausgeglichen. Der strategische Einsatz von Modulation und Stimmengruppierung in verschiedenen Registern erinnert an Schubert—aber den Schubert der Kammermusik und des Solo-Liedes, nicht des mehrstimmigen Liedes. Das letzte Werk in der Cornelius-Gruppe, seine letzte Komposition, ist vollendeter, ohne dabei die Wärme und den Schwung seiner frühen mehrstimmigen Lieder zu verlieren.

Bruckners Lieder für gemischten Chor lassen in ihrem kleinen Rahmen schon die transzendentale Qualität, Größe und Selbstsicherheit erkennen, die für seine Kirchenmusik so typisch ist. Sein Entwurf für das bisher unveröffentlichte *Du bist wie eine Blume* mit seinen Versuchen einer diffusen Mittelpartie zeigt, wie Bruckner damit kämpfte, die Proportionen dieses zarten Stückes beizubehalten und dabei gleichzeitig seiner Inspiration genügend Freiheit zu gewähren. Von den in dieser Sammlung vertretenen Komponisten ist Brahms eindeutig der bedeutendste und originellste auf dem Gebiet des Liedes für gemischten Chor und überhaupt der Chormusik im allgemeinen. Zu seiner Kenntnis der mehrstimmigen Lieder Mendelssohns und besonders Schumanns kam Brahms' lebenslanges Interesse an der Volksmusik und frühen Polyphonie. Wie die meisten seiner mehrstimmigen Lieder lassen auch die sechs Stücke in dieser Sammlung einen oder mehrere dieser unterschiedlichen Einflüsse erkennen. Das zuletzt komponierte Stück, eine Vertonung des Gedichtes *Im Herbst* von Klaus Groth, zeigt, wie Brahms genau wie in seiner unbegleiteten Kirchenmusik fein gewobene Mehrstimmigkeit mit einer ausdrucksvollen Gesamtform, Harmonie, und Materialentwicklung vereinbart.

Die mehrstimmigen Lieder von Wolf und Schoenberg in dieser Sammlung stammen alle aus den frühen Jahren ihrer Komponisten. Gegen Ende des 19. Jahrhunderts gab es eine zunehmende Tendenz, unbegleitete Chormusik (sowohl sakral als auch säkular) für professionellere Chöre zu schreiben. Wolfs Vertonung von Eichendorff-Texten als *Sechs geistliche Lieder* (1881) verdeutlicht diesen Trend, und Schoenbergs *Friede auf Erden* (1907) verkörpert ihn. Im Gegensatz dazu bieten die drei Stücke des siebzehnjährigen Wolf keine Schwierigkeiten: Sie sind eindeutig für kleinere Laienaufführungen bestimmt und fest in der romantischen Tradition verwurzelt. Schoenbergs überschäumende Vertonung des plattdeutschen Textes entstand, als der gerade Zwanzigjährige mit verschiedenen Chorvereinigungen in Wien in Verbindung stand.

Durch die Werke von Komponisten wie Paul Hindemith, Anton Webern, Hans Pfitzner, Richard Strauss, Ernst Pepping, und Hugo Distler wurde die Tradition des deutschen mehrstimmigen Liedes im späteren 20. Jahrhundert fortgeführt und seine Grenzen erweitert. Aber diese Erweiterung führte oft zu einem Verlust des Schwungs und der Spontaneität des mehrstimmigen Liedes des frühen 19. Jahrhunderts, und genau diese Eigenschaften in Verbindung mit ihrem erfrischenden romantischen Idealismus machen den Reiz dieser deutschen mehrstimmigen Lieder aus dem 19. Jahrhundert für die Sänger und Zuhörer heute aus.

Abschließend möchte ich mich für die Hilfe der folgenden Institutionen und Einzelpersonen bedanken: Die Angestellten der British Library in

London und der Österreichischen Nationalbibliothek in Wien haben mir den Zugang zu sonst nicht verfügbaren Werken von Cornelius, Franz, Gade, Loewe, und Spohr ermöglicht. Die Verwaltung der Universität Liverpool trug mit einem kleinen Stipendium dazu bei, die Kosten der anfänglichen Materialsammlung für dieses Projekt zu decken. Dank schulde ich auch Dr Robert Danbury, Miss Elizabeth Danbury, und Mr Bill Fox für ihre Hilfe bei Fragen der deutschen Grammatik; Herrn Professor Gotthilf Ehninger und Frau Renate Beck-Ehninger für Hintergrundinformationen und Einzelheiten der Textanordung; Mr Otto und Mrs Gerda Horwich für ihre Lektüre und wörtliche Übersetzung der Cornelsen-Manuskripte sowie ihre großzügige Hilfe bei meiner Übersetzung der anderen Texte; und Mr Michael Rigelsford für seine wörtliche Übersetzung des von Schoenberg vertonten plattdeutschen Textes von Klaus Groth. Der größte Dank gebührt aber meiner Familie für ihre Geduld, gute Laune und Hilfe im Laufe meiner Arbeit; den Sängern und Sängerinnen, mit denen ich so gerne an diesen und anderen Werken gearbeitet habe; und James Denny (1908–78), Musikprofessor an der Universität Leeds, der mit solcher Weitsicht mein frühes Interesse an Kammermusik für Chor gefördert hat, und dem diese Sammlung gewidmet ist.

Übersetzung: Eva Vennebusch

JUDITH BLEZZARD
Oktober 1989

1. Chor der Engel

Angels' chorus

Johann Wolfgang von Goethe

FRANZ SCHUBERT
D440

Printed in Great Britain
OXFORD UNIVERSITY PRESS, MUSIC DEPARTMENT, WALTON STREET, OXFORD OX2 6DP

30
Christ ist er - stan - den! Freu - de dem Sterb - li - chen, den die ver - derb - li - chen,
Christ is a - ris - en! By God e - lec - ted, yea, now re - sur - rec - ted to
37
schlei - chen - den, erb - li - chen Män - gel um - wan - den. Freu - de dem Sterb - li - chen,
help the af - flic - ted es - cape their op - pres - sion. By God e - lec - ted, yea,
44
den die ver - derb - li - chen, schlei - chen - den, erb - li - chen Män - gel um - wan - den.
now re - sur - rec - ted to help the af - flic - ted es - cape_ their op - pres - sion.
50
Christ ist er - stan - den! Christ ist er - stan - den!
Christ is a - ris - en! Christ is a - ris - en!
cresc.

2. Das Grab
The grave

Johann Gaudenz von Salis-Seewis

FRANZ SCHUBERT
D643*a*

Sehr langsam [Very slowly]

2 Das Lied der Nachtigallen
tönt nicht in seinem Schoss,
der Freundschaft Rosen fallen
nur auf des Hügels Moos.

3 Verlass'ne Bräute ringen
umsonst die Hände wund,
der Waisen Klagen dringen
nicht in der Tiefe Grund!

4 Doch sonst an keinem Orte
wohnt die ersehnte Ruh;
nur durch die dunkle Pforte
geht man der Heimat zu.

5 Das arme Herz hienieden
von manchem Sturm bewegt
erlangt den wahren Frieden
nur, wo es nicht mehr schlägt.

2 The songbirds' serenading
is gone, it makes no sound,
the friendship roses fading
bestrew the mossy mound.

3 Forsaken brides are weeping,
they wring their hands in vain,
and unheard by the sleeping,
the orphans' woeful strain.

4 Yet only here can mortals
find peace, so far concealed,
and through its gloomy portals
man's homeland lies revealed.

5 The wretched heart in harness
to what life holds in store
can only find true calmness
where it shall beat no more.

3. Des Menschen Trost

Mankind's solace

Friedrich Konrad Müller von der Werra

LOUIS SPOHR
(pub. *c*.1874)

2 Und wenn der Lenz mit seiner Lust,
von uns im Herbst will scheiden gehn,
so ist die Seele sich bewusst,
dass nichts auf Erden kann bestehn!
und ist dahin die Maienpracht,
und süss die schöne Zeit verkost,
so quillt ein Sehnen noch mit Macht,
die Hoffnung ist des Menschen Trost!

3 Ach wem ein recht Gedenken blüht,
den schmerzet die Vergänglichkeit;
das Herze hassend abgemüht,
ist von dem Ziel entfernt so weit;
und wenn es endlich nun erwacht,
getäuscht am Grab in Winterfrost,
so quillt ein Sehnen noch mit Macht,
die Hoffnung ist des Menschen Trost!

2 And when the verdant lively spring
to autumn turns and life grows numb,
his soul regrets no mortal thing
its span of life can overcome!
When May in splendour must depart,
its beauty gone, its strength declined,
deep longing stirs within the heart,
for hope, yes, for hope brings solace to mankind.

3 To him in whom kind mem'ry grows,
no fleeting whims his mind engage;
the hateful heart its dolour shows,
kept from its aim by spite and rage;
and when it wakens with a start,
alas! to wint'ry grave consigned,
deep longing stirs within the heart,
for hope, yes, for hope brings solace to mankind.

4. Im Vorübergehn

In passing by

Johann Wolfgang von Goethe

CARL LOEWE
Op.81 no.1

14
- grün - det; drum sind die Blü - ten so schön ge - run - det. Ich kann nicht
grow - ing; I am con - tent here, fine blos - soms show - ing. I can - not
17
dim.
lie - beln, ich kann nicht schran - zen, musst mich nicht bre - chen, musst mich ver -
serve you, I can - not woo you, O do not pluck me, yet take me
dim.
20
f
p
- pflan - - - zen. Ich ging im Wal - de so für mich
to you.' Then as I walked through the woods so
3
f
p
24
cresc.
f
p
hin; ich war so hei - ter, wollt' im-mer wei - ter, das war mein Sinn.
still, I felt new stri - ving, my life re - vi - ving, that was my will.
cresc.
f
p

5. In der Marienkirche
In the church of the Virgin Mary

Folksong

CARL LOEWE
Op.81 no.4

- vor, die neig - ten sich, die ver - zweig - ten sich, wä-ren
bloom, they grew in - clined, then their shoots en - twined, as to -
10
cresc.
- vor, die neig-ten sich, die ver-zweig-ten sich,
bloom, they grew in-clined, then their shoots en-twined,
cresc.
- vor, die neig - ten sich, die ver - zweig - ten sich, wä-ren
bloom, they grew in - clined, then their shoots en - twined, as to -
gern ein-an - der recht nah,
- geth - er wish-ing to be,
13
dim.
cresc.
dass je - der gleich er - ken-nen könnt', zwei
by death u - ni - ted in their love, so
wä-ren gern ein-an - der recht nah, recht nah,
as to-geth - er wish-ing to be, to be,
p
cresc.
dim.
gern ein-an - der recht nah,
- geth - er wish-ing to be,
all - da, zwei Lie-ben-de ruh-ten all - da.
can see, so all who pass by there can see.
17
dim.
Lie-ben-de ruh-ten all - da, zwei Lie-ben-de ruh - ten all - da.
all who pass by there can see, so all who pass by there can see.
dim.
all - da, zwei Lie-ben-de ruh - ten all - da.
can see, so all who pass by there can see.

6. Morgengebet
Morning prayer

Josef Karl Benedikt von Eichendorff

FELIX MENDELSSOHN
Op.48 no.5

2 Ich fühle mich wie neu geschaffen,
wo ist die Sorge nun und Not?
Was gestern noch mich woll't erschlaffen,
dess schäm' ich mich im Morgenrot.

2 *I sense in me a new creation,*
where now are sorrow and distress?
The sunrise bringing inspiration,
all shameful things I now confess.

13
f
p
pp
3. Die Welt mit ih - rem Gram und Glü - cke will ich, ein Pil - ger, froh be - reit be -
3. As pil-grim, I am glad - ly go - ing through mor-tal grief and joy sub - lime, to
17
cresc.
f cresc.
sf
- tre - ten nur als ei - ne Brü - cke zu dir, Herr, ü - ber'n Strom der Zeit,
come at last to you, Lord, know-ing that life is but a bridge through time,
Zeit, zu
time, to
zu dir, Herr, ü - ber'n Strom der Zeit!
that life is but a bridge through time.
21
zu dir, zu dir, Herr, ü - ber'n Strom der Zeit!
to you, life is but a bridge through time.
dir, zu dir, zu dir, zu dir, Herr, ü - ber'n Strom der Zeit!
you, to you, Lord, know - ing life is but a bridge through time.

7. Herbstlied

Autumn song

Nikolaus Lenau

FELIX MENDELSSOHN
Op.48 no.6

wei - ne, durch den Strauch, als ob er wei - ne; Ster - be -
- ment - ing, through the trees, as though la - ment - ing; near - ex -
16
f
p
durch den Strauch, als ob er wei - - - ne; Ster - be -
through the trees, as though la - ment - - ing; near - ex -
f
p
fuhr durch den Strauch, als ob er wei - ne;
howls through the trees, as though la - ment - ing;
- seuf - zer der Na - tur schau - ern durch die wel - ken Hai - ne, durch die
- haust - ed, na - ture palls, fa - cing au - tumn un - re - lent - ing, fa - cing
19
p sempre
f
- seuf - zer der Na - tur schau - ern durch die wel - ken Hai - ne,
- haust - ed, na - ture palls, fa - cing au - tumn un - re - lent - ing,
p sempre
wel - ken, durch die wel - ken Hai - ne.
au - tumn, au - tumn un - re - lent - ing.
23
dim.
p
f
espress.
durch_ die wel - ken Hai - ne. Wie - der ist, wie bald, wie
un - re - lent - ing au - tumn. O how soon it comes, a -
mir ein
Yet a-
Tempo
Fra - gend rauscht es durch den
Through the wood its ques - tions
28
sf
p rit.
pp
bald! mir ein Jahr da - hin ge - schwun - den.
- las! Yet a - no - ther year is flee - ing.
sf
mir ein
Yet a-

Wald: hat dein Herz sein Glück ge - fun - den?
pass: 'Are you hap - py, in - ner be - ing?'
32
cresc.
pp
Fra - gend rauscht es durch den Wald: hat dein Herz sein Glück ge -
Through the wood its ques-tions pass: 'Are you hap-py, in - ner
cresc.
pp
Fra - gend rauscht es durch den Wald:
Through the wood its ques-tions pass:
35
f
sf pp
- fun - den? durch den Wald: hat dein Herz sein Glück ge - fun - den?
be - ing?' Ques-tions pass: 'Are you hap - py, in - ner be - ing?'
f
sf pp
Fra - gend rauscht es durch den Wald:
Through the wood its ques-tions pass:
[♪ = 𝅗𝅥] Allegro
39
mf
sf
cresc.
Wal - des - rau-schen, wun - der - bar hast du mir das Herz ge -
For - est mur-murs, e - ver true, tell my heart so long mis -
mf
sf
cresc.
43
f
p
- trof - fen! Treu - lich bringt ein je - des Jahr neu - es Laub wie neu - es
- ta - ken: Ev - 'ry year comes life a - new, spring-time blooms fresh hopes a -
f
p

47
Laub wie neu - es
blooms fresh hopes a -
f
p
Hof - fen, treu - lich bringt ein je - des Jahr neu - es Laub, neu - es
- wa - ken, ev - 'ry year comes life a - new, spring-time blooms, spring-time
f
p
Hof - fen, neu - es
- wa - ken, spring-time
Wal - des -
For - est
51
sf
cresc.
Laub, neu - es Laub wie neu - es Hof - fen.
blooms, spring-time blooms fresh hopes a - wa - ken.
Wal - des - rau -
For - est mur -
cresc.
sf
cresc.
Wal - des -
For - est
- rau - schen, wun - der - bar
mur - murs, e - ver true,
55
f
f
- schen, wun - der - bar hast du mir das Herz ge - trof - fen! Treu - lich
- murs, e - ver true, tell my heart so long mis - ta - ken: ev - 'ry
f
f
f
- rau - schen, wun - der - bar
mur - murs, e - ver true,
neu - es
spring-time
60
p
bringt ein je - des Jahr neu - es Laub wie neu - es Hof - fen, wie
year comes life a - new, spring-time blooms fresh hopes a - wa - ken, fresh
p

Laub wie neu-es Hof-fen, wie neu - - es Hof - fen, neu - es
blooms fresh hopes a - wa-ken, fresh hopes a - wa - ken, spring-time
64
cresc.
f
neu - es, neu-es Hof - fen, wie neu - es Hof - fen,
hopes, fresh hopes a - wa - ken, fresh hopes a - wa - ken,
cresc.
Laub wie neu - es Hof - fen. Treu-lich bringt ein je - des
blooms fresh hopes a - wa - ken, ev - 'ry year comes life a -
70
dim.
p
wie neu - es Hof - fen.
fresh hopes a - wa - ken,
ne - ues Laub,
spring - time blooms,
neu - es
spring - time
Jahr, treu - lich bringt ein je - des Jahr neu - es Laub,
- new, ev - 'ry year comes life a - new, spring - time blooms,
75
neu - es Hof - - fen,
hopes a - wa - - ken,
Laub wie neu - es Hof - fen,
blooms fresh hopes a - wa - ken,
neu - es Laub,
spring-time blooms,
79
Laub, neu - es Laub wie neu - es Hof - - fen.
blooms, spring-time blooms fresh hopes a - wa - - ken.

8. Frühzeitiger Frühling

Early springtime

Johann Wolfgang von Goethe

FELIX MENDELSSOHN
Op.59 no.2

27
Bäch- lein zu - mal, sind es die Wie - sen, ist es das Tal?
flow - ing so fast, there blooms the val - ley, here springs the grass,
p
Sind es die Wie - sen, ist
there blooms the val - ley, here
33
p
cresc.
pp
Sind es die Wie - sen, ist es das Tal, ist es das Tal?
there blooms the val - ley, here springs the grass, here springs the grass,
pp
cresc.
rit.
es das Tal?
springs the grass.
39
mf
das Tal? Bläu - li - che Fri - sche! Him - mel und Höh'!
the grass. Hea - ven - ly fresh - ness! Blue is the sky!
mf
45
p
cresc.
Gol-de - ne Fi - sche wim-meln im See. Bun - tes Ge - fie - der rau - schet im
Fish in the lake teem ra - pid - ly by. Ra - di - ant plu - mage darts through the
p
cresc.

himm-li-sche Lie -
hea-ven-ly bird -
52
cresc.
sf
f
Hain; himm - li-sche Lie - der schal-len dar - ein,
wood, hea - ven-ly bird - song cap-tures the mood,
cresc.
sf
- der schal-len dar - ein,
- song cap-tures the mood,
bun- tes Ge -
ra - di - ant
59
p
p
himm-li-sche Lie - der schal-len dar - ein,
hea-ven-ly bird - song cap-tures the mood,
f
p
p
bun-tes Ge -
ra - di - ant
- fie - der
plu - mage
66
- fie - der rau - schet im Hain; himm-li-sche Lie - der schal-len dar - ein,
plu - mage darts through the wood, hea-ven-ly bird - song cap-tures the mood,
p
- fie - der
plu - mage
rit.
himm - li - sche Lie - der schal - len dar -
hea - ven - ly bird - song cap - tures the
73
p
cresc.
pp
himm- li-sche Lie - der schal- len dar - ein, schal- len dar - ein, dar -
hea- ven-ly bird - song cap- tures the mood, cap- tures the mood, the
pp
cresc.

[♩. = ♩]
S.
A.
T.
B.
- ein. Un - ter des Grü - nen blü - hen - der Kraft na - schen die
mood. Un - der the ver - dant leaves of the trees, steal - ing the
- ein. Un - ter des Grü - nen blü - hen - der Kraft
mood. Un - der the ver - dant leaves of the trees,
Bie - nen sum - mend am Saft, na - schen die Bie - nen sum - mend am
nec - tar, loud hum the bees, steal - ing the nec - tar, loud hum the
na - schen die Bie - nen sum - mend am Saft, sum - mend am
steal - ing the nec - tar, loud hum the bees, loud hum the
na - schen die Bie - nen sum - mend am
steal - ing the nec - tar, loud hum the
cresc.
dim.
Saft. Lei - se Be - we - gung bebt in der Luft, rei - zen - de Re - gung, schlä - fern - der
bees. Soft - ly the ze - phyrs waft through the air, rap - tur - ous move - ments, fra - gran - ces
Saft. Lei - se Be - we - gung bebt in der Luft, rei - zen - de
bees. Soft - ly the ze - phyrs waft through the air, rap - tur - ous
Saft. Lei - se Be - we - gung bebt in der Luft,
bees. Soft - ly the ze - phyrs waft through the air,

91
pp
Duft, rei - zen - de Re - gung, schlä-fern-der Duft, schlä -
rare, rap - tur - ous move-ments, fra - gran-ces rare, fra -
pp
Duft, schlä - - fern-der Duft, schlä -
rare, fra - - gran-ces rare, fra -
pp
Re - gung, schlä-fern-der Duft, schlä-fern-der Duft,
move-ments, fra - gran-ces rare, fra - gran-ces rare,
pp
in der Luft, rei-zen-de Re - gung, schlä-fern-der
through the air, rap-tur-ous move-ments, fra - gran-ces
95
- - fern - der Duft.
- - gran - ces rare.
cresc.
- - fern - der Duft. Mäch - ti - ger rüh - ret bald sich ein
- - gran - ces rare. Pow - er - ful bree - zes sud - den - ly
cresc.
schlä - fern - der Duft. Mäch - ti - ger rüh - ret bald sich ein
fra - gran - ces rare. Pow - er - ful bree - zes sud - den - ly
Duft.
rare.
99
cresc.
f
sf
Mäch-ti-ger rüh - ret bald sich ein Hauch,
Pow - er-ful bree - zes sud - den-ly rush,
cresc.
f
Hauch, bald sich ein
rush, sud - den - ly
cresc.
f
Hauch. Mäch-ti-ger rüh - ret bald sich ein
rush. Pow - er-ful bree - zes sud - den - ly
f
Mäch-ti-ger rüh - ret bald sich ein
Pow - er-ful bree - zes sud - den - ly

103
pp
— doch er ver - lie - ret gleich sich im Strauch,
— lo - sing them - selves at once in the bush,
cresc.
Hauch, doch er ver - lie - ret gleich sich im Strauch, mäch - ti - ger
rush, lo - sing them - selves at once in the bush, pow - er - ful
Hauch, doch er ver - lie - ret gleich sich im Strauch, mäch - ti - ger
rush, lo - sing them - selves at once in the bush, pow - er - ful
106
S.
A.
T.
B.
doch er ver - lie - ret gleich sich im
lo - sing them - selves at once in the
dim.
f
p
rüh - ret bald sich ein Hauch,
bree - zes sud - den - ly rush,
doch er ver -
lo - sing them -
109
Strauch, doch er ver - lie - ret gleich sich im Strauch, gleich sich im Strauch, gleich sich im
bush, lo - sing them-selves at once in the bush, once in the bush, once in the
dim.
cresc.
3
- lie - ret gleich sich im Strauch.
- selves, lo - sing them - selves.

113
Strauch.
bush.
[♩ = ♩.] f
A - ber zum Bu - sen kehrt er zu - rück. Hel - fet, ihr
Yet in my heart they blow to me here. Help me, O
f
119
f
p
Mu - sen, tra - gen das Glück! Sa - get seit ge - stern wie mir ge -
mu - ses, for - tune to bear! Tell me what chan - ges with the new
f
p
125
cresc.
f
Lieb - li - che
Yes, dear - est
- schah? Sa - get seit ge - stern wie mir ge - schah?
year, tell me what chan - ges with the new year.
cresc.
Schwe - stern, Lieb - chen ist da!
sis - ters, my love is here.
131
p
Lieb - li - che Schwe - stern, Lieb - chen ist
Yes, dear - est sis - ters, my love is
f
p

137
Sa - get seit ge - stern
Tell me what chan - ges
wie mir ge - schah? Lieb - li - che
da! with the new year. Yes, dear - est
here.
Sa - get seit ge - stern
Tell me what chan - ges
143
Sa - get seit ge - stern wie mir ge -
Tell me what chan - ges with the new
Schwe - stern, Lieb-chen ist da!
sis - ters, my love is here!
Lieb - li - che
Yes, dear - est
dolce
Sa - get seit ge - stern wie mir ge -
Tell me what chan - ges with the new
- schah, wie mir ge - schah, wie mir ge - schah?
149 year, with the new year, with the new year.
-schah, wie mir ge - schah, mir ge - schah? Lieb - li - che
year, with the new year, the new year. Yes, dear - est
Schwe - stern, Lieb - chen ist da!
sis - ters, my love is here,
- schah, wie mir ge - schah? Lieb - li - che
year, with the new year. Yes, dear - est
rit.
Lieb - li - che Schwe - stern, Lieb - chen ist da!
Yes, dear - est sis - ters, my love is here!
155 dolce
cresc.
Schwe-stern, lieb - li - che Schwe-stern, Lieb- chen ist da, ist da!
sis - ters, yes, dear - est sis - ters, my love is here, is here!
cresc.

9. Abschied vom Wald

Farewell to the forest

Josef Karl Benedikt
von Eichendorff

FELIX MENDELSSOHN
Op.59 no.3

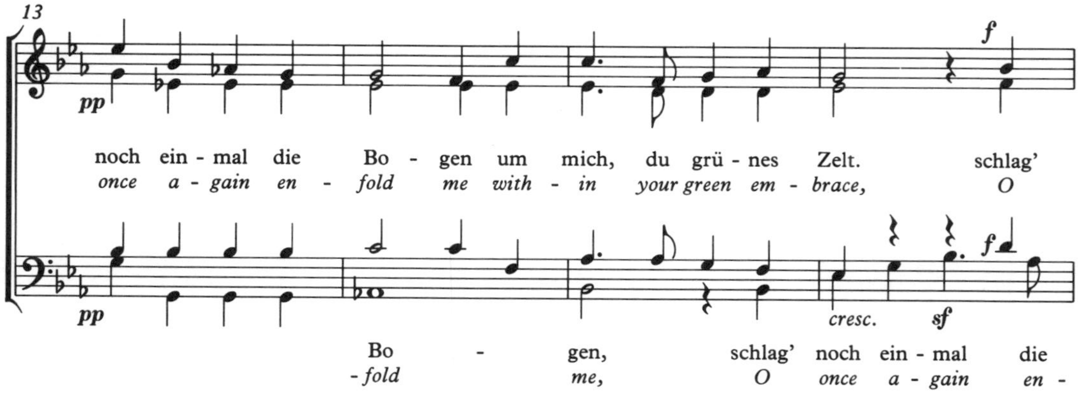

2 Im Walde steht geschrieben
ein stilles ernstes Wort
vom rechten Tun und Lieben,
und was des Menschen Hort.
Ich habe treu gelesen
die Worte, schlicht und wahr,
und durch mein ganzes Wesen
ward's unaussprechlich klar.

3 Bald werd' ich dich verlassen,
fremd in die Fremde geh'n,
auf buntbewegten Gassen
des Lebens Schauspiel seh'n.
Und mitten in dem Leben
wird deines Ernst's Gewalt
mich Einsamen erheben,
so wird mein Herz nicht alt.

2 The woodland holds great precepts
in thoughts that spring to mind
of righteousness, devotion,
the values of mankind.
These precepts I consider
serious and sincere,
they colour my existence
with guidance firm and clear.

3 So soon now I must leave you,
on journeys yet unknown,
life's dramas teem around me,
but still I stand alone.
And in the midst of life
I think of your precepts bold,
exalting me from grief,
so my heart cannot grow old.

10. Ruhetal
Valley of rest

Johann Ludwig Uhland

FELIX MENDELSSOHN
Op.59 no.5

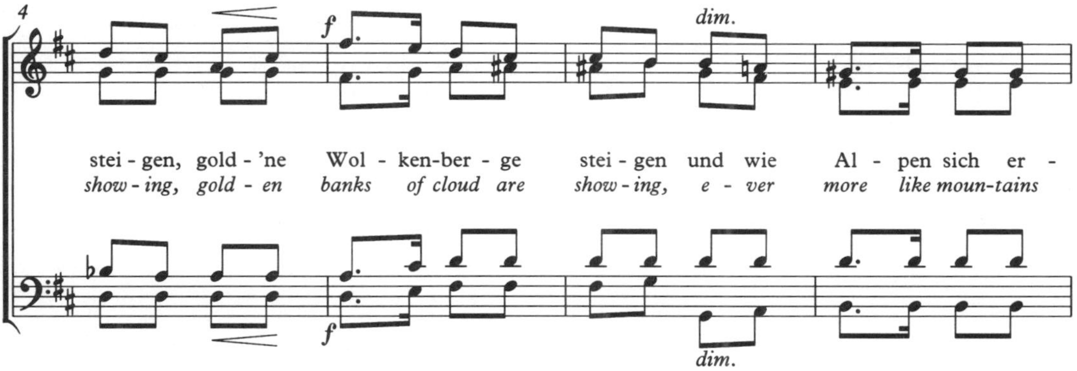

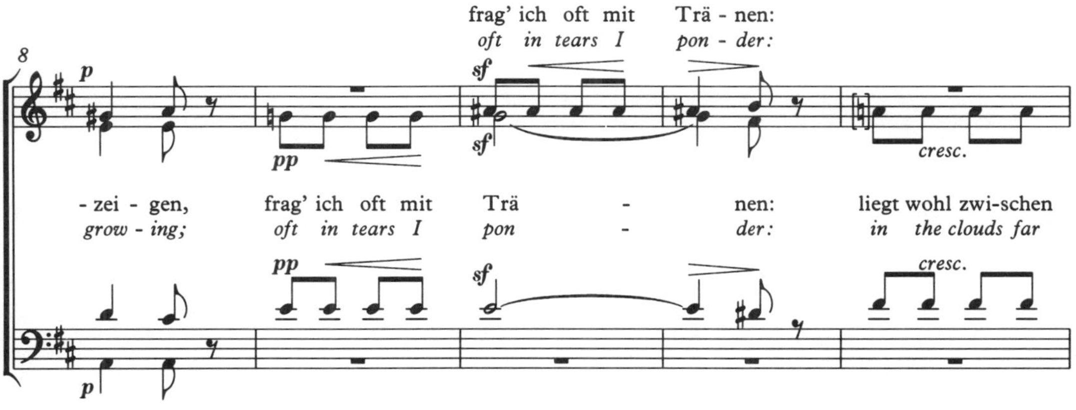

liegt wohl zwi-schen je - nen
in the clouds far yon - der
13
sf cresc. f pp
sf
je - - nen mein er - sehn - tes Ru - he - tal?
yon - - der lies my longed - for vale of rest?
sf pp
pp
mein er - sehn - tes
lies my longed - for
19
cresc. sf
frag' ich oft mit Trä - nen: liegt wohl zwi-schen
Oft in tears I pon - der: in the clouds far
liegt wohl zwi-schen, zwi - schen
in the clouds far yon - der,
cresc. sf f
frag' ich oft mit Trä - nen: liegt wohl zwi-schen je - -
Oft in tears I pon - der: in the clouds far yon - -
liegt wohl
23
f pp p Lies it
je - nen
yon - der
mein er - sehn - tes Ru - he - tal,
lies my longed - for vale of rest.
je - nen mein er - sehn - tes Ru - he-
yon - der lies my longed-for vale of
pp p
pp
- nen mein er - sehn - tes
- der lies my longed - for
dort
29 there,
cresc. sf pp
-tal, mein er - sehn - tes Ru - he - tal, mein er - sehn - tes Ru - he - tal?
rest, lies my longed-for vale of rest, lies my longed-for vale of rest?
cresc. pp
sf

11. Jägerlied

Huntsman's song

Eduard Mörike

ROBERT SCHUMANN
Op.59 no.3

17
sf
_ ein Brief-lein mir in's fer - ne Land. In die Lüf - te hoch ein Rei-her steigt,
_ she writes to me in dis - tant land. In the air a he - ron soar-ing high,
sf
24
fp
da - hin we - der Pfeil noch Ku - gel fleugt: tau - send mal so hoch und
climbs where nei - ther shot nor ar - rows fly: yet a thou-sand times as
fp
die Ge-dan-ken
swift-er yet can
30
fp
so ge-schwind, tau - send mal so hoch und so ge-schwind, die Ge-
high a - bove, yet a thou-sand times as high a - bove, swift-er
fp
treu - er Lie - be sind,
fly our thoughts of love,
rit.
37
- dan - ken treu - er Lie-be, die Ge - dan - ken treu - er Lie - be sind!
yet can fly our love, swift-er yet can fly our thoughts of love!

12. John Anderson

Robert Burns
trans. Wilhelm Gerhard

ROBERT SCHUMANN
Op.67 no.5

13. Der Rekrut
The recruit

Robert Burns
trans. Wilhelm Gerhard

ROBERT SCHUMANN
Op.75 no.4

21
p
2. Stutz' dei - nen Bi - ber und_ stutz' mir ihn fein, 'sgeht ü - ber die
3. Pfei - fen die Ku - geln dir__ um das Ge - sicht, so denk' an dein
2. Cock up your bea - ver, and_ cock it full spruce; we'll o - ver the
3. Bul - lets are whist - ling, they_ fly past your head, but think of your
p
26
Gren - ze durch feind - li - che Reih'n! Dort pfei - fen die Ku - geln hin -
Mäd - chen, und_ fürch - te dich nicht! Und bringst auch 'nen Hieb mit auf der
bor - der and_ give_ them a brush; there's some - bo - dy there we'll teach_
sweet - heart and_ don't be a - fraid! And if your cheek's wound - ed where the
31
fp
- ü - ber, her - ü - ber, juch - hei bra - ver John - nie, stutz' auf dei - nen
Wan - ge quer - ü - ber, juch - hei bra - ver John - nie, ich__ hab' dich_ nur
bet - ter be - ha - viour, hoo - ray, my brave John - nie lad,_ cock up___ your
bul - lets have bruised you, hoo - ray, my brave John - nie, the__ more I___ will
fp
36
cresc.
f
Bi - ber, juch - hei bra - ver John - nie, stutz' auf dei - nen Bi - ber!
lie - ber, juch - hei bra - ver John - nie, ich__ hab' dich_ nur lie - ber!
bea - ver, hoo - ray, my brave John - nie lad,_ cock up___ your bea - ver!
love you, hoo - ray, my brave John - nie, the__ more I___ will love you!
cresc.
f

14. Der Schmidt

The blacksmith

Johann Ludwig Uhland

ROBERT SCHUMANN
Op.145 no.1

18
geh' ich vor - ü - ber, die Bäl - ge dann sau - sen, die Flam-men auf - brau-sen und
as I pass near him the bel - lows are wheez-ing, the flames are in - creas-ing, the
24
ich
I
lo - dern um ihn. Ich hör' mei-nen Schatz, den Ham-mer er schwin-get,
fire_ is a - blaze. I hear my de - light, his ham - mer is swing - ing, er
is
fp
fp
ihn.___ Ich hör' mei-nen Schatz, den Ham - mer er
- blaze.___ I hear my de - light, his ham - mer is
hör' mei-nen Schatz, den Ham-mer er___ schwin-get, das rau - schet, das
hear my de - light, his ham - mer is___ swing - ing, the roar - ing, the
30
p
fp
schwin-get, den Ham - mer er schwin - get, das rau - schet und klin - get, das
swing - ing, his ham - mer is swing - ing, the roar - ing and ring - ing from
p
fp
klin - get, das dringt in die Wei - te wie Glo - cken - ge - läu - te durch
ring - ing from far off re - bound - ing like bell - chimes___ re - sound - ing through
35
fp
cresc.
ff
dringt in die Wei - te, wie Glo - cken, wie Glo - cken,___ wie Glo-cken - ge -
far off re - bound - ing like bell-chimes, like bell - chimes,_ like bell-chimes re -
fp
cresc.
ff

Gas - sen und Platz. Ich hör' mei-nen Schatz, das rau - schet und klin-get, das
al - ley and street. I hear my de - light, the roar - ing and ring-ing, the
41
fp
cresc.
- läu - te. Ich hör' mei-nen Schatz, das rau - schet und klin - get, das dringt in die
- sound-ing. I hear my de - light, the roar - ing and ring - ing from far off re -
fp
cresc.
47
f
p
klin - get wie
ring - ing like
Glo - cken - ge - läu - te durch Gas - sen und Platz. Ich hör' mei-nen
Wei - te wie
bell-chimes re - sound-ing through al - ley and street. I hear my de-
- bound-ing like
f
p
das rau - schet, das klin - get, das dringt
the roar - ing, the ring - ing from far
53
dim.
Schatz, den Ham-mer er schwin-get,
-light, his ham - mer is swing - ing,
das rau - schet, das dringt
the roar - ing from far
dim.
in die Wei - te wie Glo - cken - ge - läu - te,
off re - bound - ing like bell - chimes re - sound - ing,
59
pp
— in die Wei - te wie Glo - cken-ge - läu - te, ich hör' mei-nen Schatz.
— off re - bound - ing like bell - chimes re - sound - ing, I hear my de - light.
pp

15. Sommerlied
Summer song

Friedrich Rückert | ROBERT SCHUMANN
Op.146 no.4

15
Wo ist dein Kranz,_ Mai? wohnt dir kein Glanz bei, wohnt dir kein Glanz bei, wenn der
May flowers so ten - der, where is your splen-dour, where is your splen-dour, when_ love's
19
cresc. dim. pp pp
Lie - be, der Lie - be Son - nen-schein zer - rann, zer - rann?_ Nach - ti-gall,1
sun-shine, love's sun-shine melts in tears a - way, a - way?_ Night - in-gale,
24
schwing' dich laut mit Schall; bring' mich ab, hin-ab zur Ros' in's Grab,
wake me with your song, take me to the tomb where ro - ses bloom,
28
bring' mich zur Ros' hin - ab in's Grab, zur Ros' hin - ab in's Grab.
show me the tomb where ro - ses bloom, the tomb where ro - ses bloom.

16. Es ist ein Schnee gefallen

A fall of snow

Folksong

ROBERT FRANZ
Op.24 no.1

11
zer -
its
cresc.
Haus hat kei - nen Gie - bel, es ist mir wor - den alt, zer - bro - chen
house now lacks a ga - ble, I fear it is grown old, its locks are
cresc.
cresc.
es ist mir ge-wor - den alt, zer - bro -
I fear it is grow - ing old, its locks
- bro - chen sind mir die Rie - gel, mein Stüb - lein ist mir
locks are bro-ken, un - a - ble to keep out win - ter's
15
cresc.
p
p
sind mir die Rie - gel, mein Stüb - lein ist mir
bro - ken, un - a - ble to keep out win - ter's
p
- chen sind mir die Rie - gel,
are bro-ken, un - a - ble
kalt.
cold.
19
con anima
mf
pp
kalt, ist mir kalt. Ach Lieb, lass dich's er - bar - men, dass
cold, win - ter's cold. Ah, would that love would bless me, for
pp
mf
kalt.
cold.

und schliess' mich in dei - ne
and here in her arms em -
23
ich so e - lend bin, und schliess' mich in dei - ne
sor - row fills my heart, and here in her arms em -
und schliess' mich in dei - ne
and here in her arms em -
Ar - me, in dei - ne Ar - me, so fährt der Win - ter
- brace me, her arms em - brace me, then win - ter would de -
26
Ar - me, in dei - ne Ar - me,
- brace me, her arms em - brace me,
so fährt der Win - ter
then win - ter would de -
Ar - me, in dei - ne Ar - me, so fährt, so
- brace me, her arms em - brace me, then win - ter
hin, so fährt der Win - ter hin.
- part, then win - ter would de - part.
30
f
so fährt der Win - ter da - hin.
then win - ter would de - part.
hin, so fährt der Win - ter, der Win - ter hin.
- part, then win - ter would de - part, it would de - part.
fährt, so fährt der Win - ter hin.
would, then win - ter would de - part.

17. Ave Maria

Emanuel Geibel

ROBERT FRANZ
Op.45 no.1

Ruhig und getragen, doch nicht zu langsam [Calm and sustained, but not too slow]

7
Tun, zur Jung-frau be-tet, zu der Jung-frau Sohn; des Him-mels Schaa-ren sel - ber
free, now pray-ing to the Ho-ly Vir-gin's Son; the mul-ti-tudes of hea - ven
Tun, o be - tet zu der Jung-frau Sohn; des Him - mels Schaa - ren
free, now pray - ing to the Vir-gin's Son; the hosts of hea - ven
Tun, zur Jung-frau be-tet, zu der Jung - frau Sohn; des Him-mels Schaa-ren sel - ber
free, now pray-ing to_ the Ho-ly Vir - gin's Son; the mul-ti-tudes of hea - ven
Tun, o be-tet zu der Jung-frau Sohn; des Him - mels Schaa - ren
free, now pray-ing to the Vir-gin's Son; the hosts of hea - ven
10
knie - en nun mit Li - lien-stä-ben vor des Va - ters Thron, und
kneel - ing down with li - ly wands be-fore the Fa - ther's throne, and
knie - en nun, knie'n vor des Va - ters Thron, nun
kneel - ing down be - fore the Fa - ther's throne, now
knie - en nun mit Li - lien-stä-ben vor des Va - ters Thron,
kneel - ing down with li - ly wands be-fore the Fa - ther's throne,
knie - en nun mit Li - lien-stä - ben vor des_ Va-ters Thron,
kneel - ing down with li - ly wands be - fore the_ Fa-ther's throne,
13
cresc.
durch die Ro-sen-wol-ken wehn die Lie-der der sel'-gen Gei-ster fei-er-lich her-nie -
through the ro-sy clouds come songs a - bound-ing from bless-ed spi-rits to the earth re-sound -
cresc.
we - hen, we - hen Lie-der der sel'-gen Gei-ster nie - -
bless - ed songs are sound-ing from bless-ed spi-rits sound - -
cresc.
sel' - ge Lie - der we-hen fei - er - lich her - nie -
bless - ed songs are sound-ing to_ the earth re - sound -
cresc.
sel' - ge Lie - der we-hen fei - er - lich her - nie -
bless - ed songs are sound-ing to the earth re - sound -

16
- der. O heil'ge An - dacht, wel-che je - des
- ing. O ho - ly pray - er, how you move men's
- der, sel' - ge Lie - der weh'n her - nie - der. O heil'ge An - dacht, wel-che je - des
- ing, bless - ed songs to earth re-sound-ing. O ho - ly pray - er, how you move men's
- der, sel' - ge Lie - der weh'n her - nie - der. O heil'ge An - dacht, wel-che je - des
- ing, bless - ed songs to earth re-sound - ing. O ho - ly pray - er, how you move men's
- der, sie weh'n her - nie - der. O heil'ge An - dacht, wel-che je - des
- ing, to earth re - sound-ing. O ho - ly pray - er, how you move men's
20
Herz mit lei - sen Schau - ern wun - der - bar durch-dringt.
hearts with gen - tle stir - rings that de - vo - tion brings.
Herz leis' schau - ernd wun - der - bar durch - dringt.
hearts with stir - rings that de - vo - tion brings.
Herz mit lei - sen Schau - ern wun - der - bar durch - dringt. O heil' - ger,
hearts with gen - tle stir - rings that de - vo - tion brings. O ho - ly,
Herz leis' schau - ernd wun - der - bar durch - dringt. O heil' - ger,
hearts with stir - rings that de - vo - tion brings. O ho - ly,
22
O heil'ger Glau - be, der sich him - mel - wärts auf des Ge - be - tes wei - ssem
O ho - ly faith, which to heav'n de - parts and soars a - loft to God on
O heil'ger Glau - be, der sich him - mel - wärts auf wei - ssem Fit - tig
O ho - ly faith, which to heav'n de - parts and soars to God on
O heil'ger Glau - be, der sich him - mel - wärts auf des Ge - be - tes wei-ssem
O ho - ly faith, which to heav'n de - parts and soars a - loft to God on
heil' - ger Glau - be, der sich him - mel - wärts auf wei - ssem Fit - tig
ho - ly faith, which to heav'n de - parts and soars to God on

25
Fit - tig schwingt! In mil - de Trä-nen löst sich da der Schmerz, in -
prayer's white wings! Soft tears as-suage the grief that pain im - parts, a
be - tend schwingt! In Trä - nen löst sich da der Schmerz, in -
prayer's white wings! As - suage the grief that pain im - parts, a
Fit - tig schwingt! In mil - de Trä-nen löst sich da der Schmerz, in -
prayer's white wings! Soft tears as-suage the grief that pain im - parts, a
be - tend schwingt! In Trä - nen löst sich da der Schmerz, in -
prayer's white wings! As - suage the grief that pain im - parts, a
28
pp
- dess der Freu-de Ju - bel sanf - ter klingt. A - ve Ma - ri - a!
joy - ful note of glad - ness gent - ly rings.
- dess die Freu - de sanf - ter klingt. A - ve Ma - ri - a!
note of glad - ness gent - ly rings.
- dess der Freu-de Ju - bel sanf - ter klingt. A - ve Ma - ri - a!
joy - ful note of glad - ness gent - ly rings.
- dess die Freu - de sanf - ter klingt. A - ve Ma - ri - a!
note of glad - ness gent - ly rings.
31
p
Wenn die Glo - cke tö-net, so lä - cheln Erd' und Him - mel mild ver - söh - net.
Hear the bell re - ci-ting, and now is earth with heav'n in peace u - ni - ting.
Wenn die Glo - cke tö-net, lacht Erd' und Him - mel mild ver - söh - net.
Hear the bell re - ci-ting, now earth and heav'n in peace u - ni - ting.
Wenn die Glo - cke tö-net, lacht Erd' und Him-mel mild ver - söh - net.
Hear the bell re - ci-ting, now earth and heav'n in peace u - ni - ting.
Wenn die Glo - cke tö-net, lacht Erd' und Him-mel mild ver - söh - net.
Hear the bell re - ci-ting, now earth and heav'n in peace u - ni - ting.

18. Er ist's!
'Tis he!

Eduard Mörike

ROBERT FRANZ
Op.53 no.2

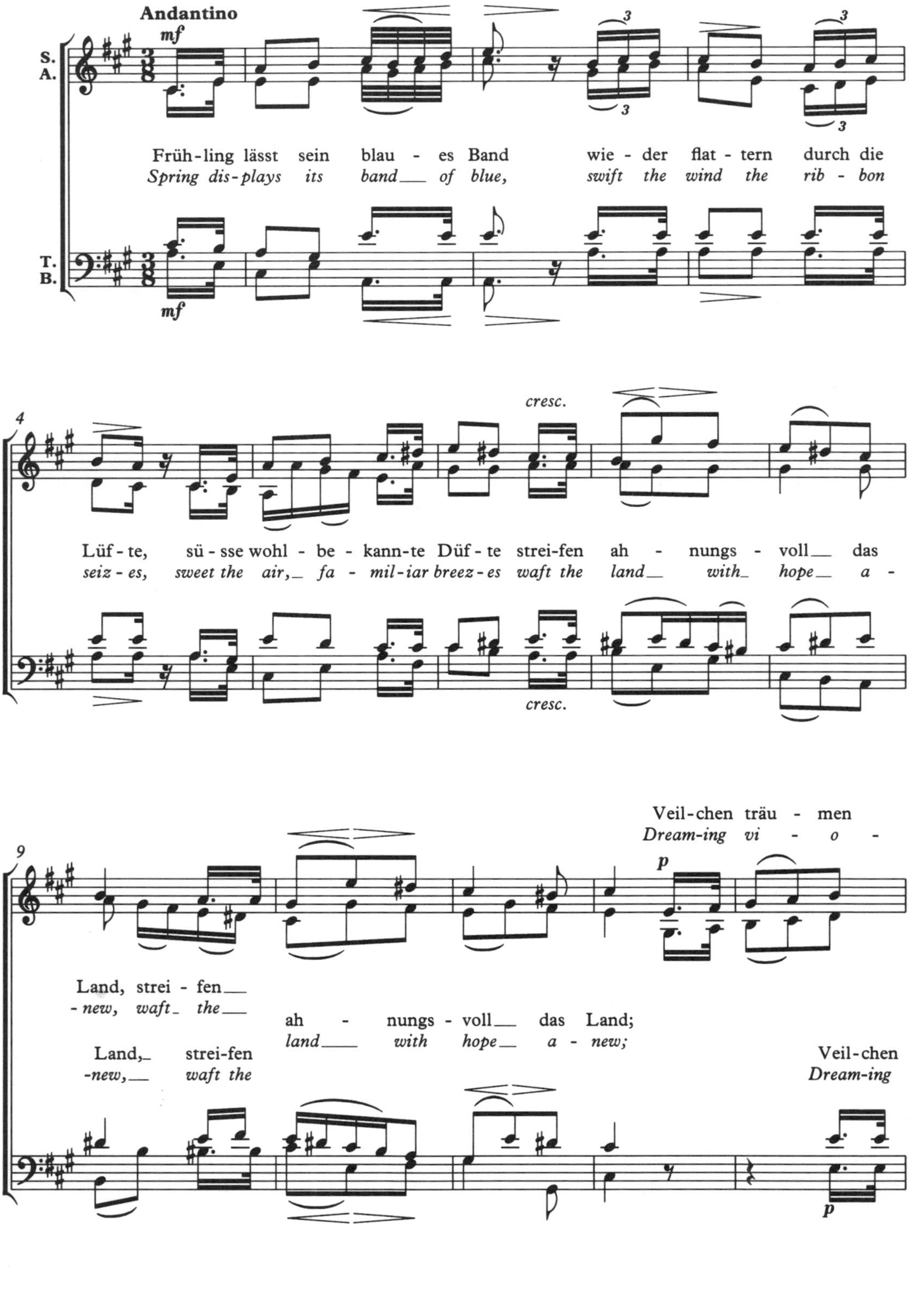

schon, wol-len bal - de kom - men; horch, von
-lets will so soon a - wa - ken; hark! from
14
p
pp
horch,
träum - en schon, wol-len bal - de kom-men; hark!
vi - o - lets will so soon a - wa - ken;
pp
fern ein lei - ser Har - fen - ton! Früh - ling, ja du bist's!
far a-way a harp's sweet notes! Spring-time, here you come!
19
mf
ein Har - fen - ton! Früh - ling, ja du bist's!
a harp's sweet notes! Spring - time, here you come!
mf
Früh - ling, ja du bist's!
Spring-time, here you come!
Früh - ling, ja du bist's! Dich hab' ich ver - nom - -
Spring-time, here you come! I was not mis - ta - -
24
cresc.
Früh - ling, ja du bist's!
Spring - time, here you come!
Dich, ja dich hab' ich ver - nom - -
I, so I was not mis - ta - -
cresc.
Früh - ling, ja du bist's! Dich hab' ich ver - nom - -
Spring-time, here you come! I was not mis - ta - -
- men,
- ken!
29
3
3
-men, dich, dich hab' ich, dich hab' ich ver - nom - men!
-ken, so I was not, I was not mis - ta - ken!
- men,
- ken,

19. Ritter Frühling

Spring, the handsome knight

Emanuel Geibel

NIELS GADE
Op.13 no.1

17
mf dim. p f
- schmie - det, den sich der Win-ter ge - schmie - det. 2. Und nun mit tri - um -
- decked him, with which the win - ter be - decked him. 2. And now with loud tri -
mf dim. p f
- schmie - det,
- decked him,
22
p
- phie-ren-dem Schall, durch-zieht er Land und Wo - gen, als He - rold kommt die
- um - phal cries o'er land and sea he's ri - ding, the night - in - gale be -
p
26
mf
Nach-ti - gall vor ihm da-her ge - flo - gen. Und rings er - schallt an
- fore him flies, sing-ing a he - rald's ti - dings. And all a - round in
mf
30
f
je - des Herz sein Auf - ruhr al - ler Or - ten, und hüllt' es sich in
ev - 'ry place, in ev - 'ry heart of mor - tal, yet though it were in
f
und hüllt' es
yet though it
öff - nen
o - pen
34
mf
drei-fach Erz es muss ihm öff - nen die Pfor - ten, es
bronze en-cased, to him must o - pen its por - tal, to
mf
sich in drei - fach Erz es muss ihm öff - nen die Pfor - ten, es
were in bronze en - cased, must o - pen to him its por - tal, to

38
S.
A.
T.
B.
dim.
p
f
muss ihm öff - nen die Pfor - ten, es muss ihm öff - nen die
him must o - pen its por - tal, to him must o - pen its
muss ihm öff - nen die Pfor - ten, es muss ihm öff - nen die
him must o - pen its por - tal, to him must o - pen its
muss ihm öff - nen die Pfor - ten, es muss ihm öff - nen die
him must o - pen its por - tal, to him must o - pen its
muss ihm öff - nen die Pfor - ten, es muss ihm öff-nen, muss ihm öff - nen die
him must o - pen its por - tal, to him must o - pen, o - pen, o - pen its
43
Pfor - ten dicht, und darf sich nim - mer ent-schuld'-gen, und muss der Kö - ni - gin, die er
por - tal strong, its door un-locked now for e - ver, the knight his no - ble queen, as cham -
Pfor-ten dicht, und darf sich nim - mer ent - schuld' - gen, und muss der
por-tal strong, its door un-locked now for e - ver, the knight his
Pfor-ten dicht, und darf sich nim - mer ent - schuld' - gen, nim - mer ent - schuld'-gen, und
por - tal strong, its door un-locked now for e - ver, now for e - ver, the
Pfor - ten dicht, und darf sich nim - mer ent-schuld' - gen, darf sich nim - mer ent -
por - tal strong, its door un-locked now for e - ver, door un - locked now for
48
rall.
pp
- ver-ficht, der Kö - ni-gin Min - ne huld' - gen.
- pi - on, as cham-pi-on, love shall fa - vour.
Kö - ni - gin, der Kö - ni-gin Min - ne huld' - gen.
no - ble queen, as cham-pi-on, love shall fa - vour.
muss der Kö - ni - gin Min - ne huld' - gen.
knight his no - ble queen, love shall fa - vour.
- schuld'-gen, muss der Kö - ni-gin Min - ne huld' - gen.
e - ver, he as cham-pi-on, love shall fa - vour.

20. Die Wasserrose
The water-lily

Emanuel Geibel

NIELS GADE
Op.13 no.2

9
pp
Kelch ist weiss wie Schnee. Da giesst der Mond vom
cha - lice white as snow. There shines the moon in
blau - - en See. Da giesst der
lake be - low. There shines the
Kelch ist weiss wie Schnee. Da giesst der Mond vom
cha - lice white as snow. There shines the moon in
p
Kelch ist weiss wie Schnee. Da giesst der Mond
cha - lice white as snow. There shines the moon,
12
Him - mel all' sei - nen gold' - nen Schein, giesst
hea - ven, send - ing its gold - en rays, out -
Mond all' sei - nen gold' - nen Schein, giesst
moon, send - ing its gold - en rays, out -
Him - mel all' sei - nen gold' - nen Schein, giesst
hea - ven, send - ing its gold - en rays, out -
all' sei - nen gold' - nen Schein, giesst
send - ing its gold - en rays, out -
15
al - le sei - ne Strah - len in ih - ren Schoss hin - ein.
- pour - ing all its bright - ness to set the flow'r a - blaze.
al - le sei - ne Strah - len in ih - ren Schoss hin - ein.
- pour-ing all its bright - ness to set the flow'r a - blaze.
al - le sei - ne Strah - len in ih - ren Schoss hin - ein.
- pour - ing all its bright - ness to set the flow'r a - blaze.
al - le sei - ne Strah - len in ih - ren Schoss hin - ein.
- pour - ing all its bright - ness to set the flow'r a - blaze.

20
pp
2. Im Was - - ser um die Blu - me
2. A - round the flo - wer swims a
pp
2. Im Was - - - ser um die Blu
2. A - round the flo - wer swims
pp
2. Im Was - ser um die Blu - me krei - set ein Schwan,
2. A - round the flo - wer swims a swan clothed in white,
pp
2. Im Was - ser um die Blu - me krei - set ein
2. A - round the flo - wer swims a swan clothed in
23
mf
p
dim.
krei - set ein wei - sser Schwan, er singt so süss, so
swan clothed in pur - est white, it sings so sweet, so
- me krei - set ein wei - - sser
a swan clothed in pur - - est
ein wei - sser Schwan, er singt so süss, so
in pur - est white, it sings so sweet, so
Schwan, ein wei - sser Schwan, er singt so süss, so
white, in pur - est white, it sings so sweet, so
27
lei - se, und schaut die Blu - me an. Er singt so süss, so
soft - ly, it keeps the flow'r in sight. It sings so sweet, so
Schwan, wei - sser Schwan. Er singt so
white, pur - est white. It sings so
lei - se, und schaut die Blu - me an. Er singt so süss, so
soft - ly, it keeps the flow'r in sight. It sings so sweet, so
lei - se, und schaut die Blu - me an. Er singt so süss,
soft - ly, it keeps the flow'r in sight. It sings so sweet,

31
p
lei - se, und will im Sin-gen ver-gehn. O Blu-me, wei - sse
soft - ly, yet soon its life has to end. O can you, pure white
lei - se, und will im Sin-gen ver-gehn. O Blu-me, wei-sse
soft - ly, yet soon its life has to end. O can you, pure white
lei - se, und im Sin-gen ver-gehn. O Blu - me,
soft - ly, yet its life has to end. O can you,
und will im Sin - gen ver - gehn. O Blu - me,
yet soon its life has to end. O can you,
35
pp
Blu - me, kannst du das Lied ver-stehn? O
flow - er, the swan's song com - pre-hend? O
Blu - me, kannst du das Lied ver -
flow - er, the swan's song com - pre -
Blu - me, kannst du das Lied ver-stehn? O
can you the swan's song com - pre-hend? O
Blu - me, kannst du das Lied ver -
can you the swan's song com - pre -
38
dim.
Blu - me, kannst du das Lied ver - stehn?
can you the swan's song com - pre - hend?
- stehn? O Blu - me, kannst du das Lied ver - stehn?
- hend? O can you the swan's song com - pre - hend?
Blu - me, kannst du das Lied ver - stehn?
can you the swan's song com - pre - hend?
- stehn? O Blu - me, kannst du das Lied ver - stehn?
- hend? O can you the swan's song com - pre - hend?

21. Der Traum
The dream

Johann Ludwig Uhland

PETER CORNELIUS (1842)

16
f
cresc.
ff
pp
- sund, sie hiel - ten sich fest um - schlun - gen, sie
- gain, em - bra - cing, and in their rap - ture be -
f
cresc.
ff
pp
19
p
wur - den jung und ge - sund. Zwei Glöck - lein klan - gen
- com - ing strong once a - gain. Two bells rang out, all
p
22
sie
she
hel - le, der Traum ver-schwand zur Stund', sie lag
dream - ing to va - nish at their sound, she lay
sie
she
25
lag
lay
cresc.
pp
in der Klo - ster - zel - le, er fern in des Tur - mes Grund.
in the con - vent's deep - est cell, his grave in the to - wer's ground.
cresc.
pp
lag
lay

22. Nichts ohne Liebe
Nothing without love

Johann Nepomuk Vogel

PETER CORNELIUS
(1842)

2 Blume nickt der Blume zu,
flüstert in des Morgens Schimmer.
Leben, ach wie schön bist du!
aber ohne Liebe, nimmer!

3 Wellen tauschen Wort um Wort,
rieseln hin in Silberflimmer,
fröhlich geht's in zweien fort,
aber ohne Liebe, nimmer!

4 Menschenherz voll Lust und Pein
fühlst wohl auch dies eine immer:
selig bist du nur allein,
aber ohne Liebe, nimmer!

2 Whisp'ring zephyrs from afar,
morning breeze sets flowers a-quiver.
Life, how beautiful you are!
yet if love is absent, never!

3 Lapping waves converse anew,
sparkling silver on the river;
gaily bounding two by two,
yet if love is absent, never!

4 Who, beset with joy and pain
could not know that he for ever
blest shall be, and he alone,
yet if love is absent, never!

23. Die Sternlein
The little stars

Ernst Moritz Arndt

PETER CORNELIUS
(1842)

2 Und die Sternlein gingen zum
lieben Mond in der Nacht,
und sie sprachen: 'Du, der auf den
Wolken trohnt in der Nacht,
lasset uns wandeln mit dir,
denn dein lieber Schein,
er verbrennt uns nimmer
die Äugelein.'
und er nahm sie, Gesellen der Nacht.

3 Nun, willkommen Sternlein und
guter Mond in der Nacht!
Ihr versteht, was still in dem
Herzen wohnt in der Nacht!
Kommt und zündet die
himmlischen Lichter mir an,
dass ich lustig mitschwärmen
und spielen kann
in der freundlichen Spielen der Nacht.

2 And the starlets, they went to the
kindly moon in the night,
And they said: 'O moon, on your
cloudy throne in the night,
let us travel with you,
for your silvery beam
will not scorch out our eyes
nor will hinder our gleam,'
so they travelled with him in the night.

3 So now welcome, O moon, with your
shimmering stars in the night,
for you know the secrets of all
our hearts in the night.
Come and kindle the
heavenly lights with your ray
so that I too may join in
your revels and play
as your friend in the games of the night.

Cornelius did not indicate the underlay for verses 2 and 3, and rhythms need to be adjusted to fit the text.

24. Aetherische Geisterstimmen
Ethereal spirit-voices

Unknown poet

PETER CORNELIUS (*c.*1842)

15
wie regt ihr mir so sü - sse
how great my heart's e - la - tion
die Brust ihr herr - li-chen
to hear your glo - ri - ous
regt ihr mir so sü - sse
great my heart's e - la - tion
die Brust ihr herr - li - chen
to hear your glo - ri - ous
18
Stim-men, wie regt ihr mir so sü - sse die Brust ihr herr-li-chen Stim-men, wie
voi - ces, how great my heart's e - la - tion to hear your glo - ri - ous voi - ces, how
Stim-men,
voi - ces,
23
regt ihr mir so sü - sse die Brust ihr herr - li-chen Stim-men.
great my heart's e - la - tion to hear your glo - ri - ous voi - ces.
[mp]
Ich
I
27
[mp]
Ich schlie-sse leis mein Aug' da ziehn Er - in - ne - run-gen,
I soft - ly close my eyes and me - mo-ries are flow - ing,
[mp]
schlie-sse leis mein Au - ge da ziehn Er - in - ne - run-gen, wie
soft - ly close my eyes and me - mo - ries are flow - ing, like

31
wie A - bend - däm - me - rung-en um-weht vom Früh - lings -
like sun - set's ro - sy glow-ing a - loft on spring - time
A - bend - däm - me - rung um - weht vom Früh - lings -
sun - set's ro - sy glow a - loft on spring - time
34
[cresc.]
- hau-che, Er - in - ne-rung, Er - in - ne - rung, Er - in - ne-rung, Er - in - ne -
breez-es, such me-mo-ries, such me-mo - ries, such me-mo-ries, such me-mo -
[cresc.]
38
[f]
- rung, Er - in - ne - rung, Er - in - ne -
- ries, such me-mo - ries, such me-mo -
[f]
[f]
Er - in - ne - rung, Er - in - ne - rung,
such me - mo - ries, such me-mo - ries,
42
[ff] con moto
- rung, Er - in - ne-rung, Er - in - ne-rung um - weht vom Früh-lings -
- ries, such me - mo-ries, such me - mo-ries a - loft on spring-time
[ff]

46
- hau - che, Er - in - ne-rung, Er - in - ne-rung um - weht vom Früh - lings -
breez - es, such me - mo-ries, such me - mo-ries a - loft on spring - time
50
Tempo 1
[mf]
- hauch, Er - in - ne-rung um-weht vom Früh-lings-hauch, Er - in - ne -
breeze, such me-mo-ries a - loft on spring-time breeze, such me - mo -
[mf]
54
- rung, Er - in - ne-rung um-weht vom Früh-lings - hauch, vom
- ries, such me - mo-ries a - loft on spring-time breeze, on
- rung, Er - in - ne-rung um-weht vom Früh - lings-hauch,
- ries, such me-mo-ries a - loft on spring - time breeze,
57
Früh - lings - hauch, um-weht vom Früh - lings - hauch.
spring - time breeze, a - loft on spring - time breeze.

25. Frühlingsglaube

Belief in springtime

Johann Ludwig Uhland — PETER CORNELIUS (1842)

Ziemlich bewegt [Somewhat agitated]

13
O frisch-er Duft,_ o neu - er Klang! nun, ar-mes Her - ze, sei nicht
Es blüht das fern - ste, tief - ste Tal! nun, ar-mes Herz,_ ver-giss die
What won-drous sounds,_ what fra - grant air! Now, bar-ren heart,_ do not des -
The fur-thest vale__ breaks in - to leaf! Now, bar-ren heart,_ for-get your
18
bang, nun, ar-mes Her - ze, sei nicht bang!
Qual, nun, ar-mes Herz,_ ver-giss die Qual! nun muss sich al - les, al - les
- pair, now, bar-ren heart,_ do not des - pair! New life is al - ways, al-ways
grief, now, bar-ren heart,_ for-get your grief!
22
rit.
molto rit.
wen - den, al - les, al - les wen - den.
grow - ing, al - ways, al - ways grow - ing.

26. Der Fichtenbaum

The fir-tree

Heinrich Heine

PETER CORNELIUS (*c.*1842)

16
S.
A.
T.
B.
mf
p
Schnee. Er träumt von ei - ner
ice. It dreams a - bout a
Schnee. Er träumt von ei - ner Pal - me, er träumt von ei - ner
ice. It dreams a - bout a palm tree, it dreams a - bout a
Schnee. Er träumt von ei - ner
ice. It dreams a - bout a
Schnee. Er träumt von ei - ner
ice. It dreams a - bout a
20
[p]
Pal - me, die, fern im Mor - gen -
palm tree of o - ri - ent a -
Pal - me, die, fern im Mor - gen - land, die, fern im Mor - gen -
palm tree of o - ri - ent a - far, of o - ri - ent a -
Pal - me, die, fern im Mor - gen -
palm tree of o - ri - ent a -
Pal - me, die, fern im Mor - gen -
palm tree of o - ri - ent a -
24
- land, ein - sam und schwei - gend trau - ert auf
- far, lone - ly and mute, la - ment - ing its
- land, ein - sam und schwei - gend trau - ert auf
- far, lone - ly and mute, la - ment - ing its
- land, ein - sam und schwei - gend
- far, lone - ly and mute, la -
- land, ein - sam und schwei - gend
- far, lone - ly and mute, la -

27
bren-nen-der Fel-sen - wand, ein-sam und schwei - gend
scorch-ing and rock - y scar, lone - ly and mute, la -
bren-nen-der Fel - sen - wand,
scorch-ing and rock - y scar,
trau - ert auf bren-nen-der Fel - sen - wand, ein-sam und
- ment - ing its scorch-ing and rock - y scar, lone - ly, la -
trau - ert auf bren-nen-der Fel - sen - wand, ein-sam und
- ment - ing its scorch-ing and rock - y scar, lone - ly, la -
31
ff
trau - ert auf bren - nen - der Fel - sen - wand,
- ment - ing its scorch - ing and rock - y scar,
ein - sam und schwei - gend auf bren - nen - der Fel - sen - wand,
lone - ly, la - ment - ing its scorch - ing and rock - y scar,
schwei - gend auf bren - nen - der Fel - sen - wand,
- ment - ing its scorch - ing and rock - y scar,
schwei - gend auf bren - nen - der Fel - sen - wand,
- ment - ing its scorch - ing and rock - y scar,
34
p
auf bren - nen - der Fel - sen - wand.
its scorch - ing and rock - y scar.
ein - sam und schwei-gend auf bren - nen - der Fel - sen - wand.
palm tree, la - ment - ing its scorch - ing and rock - y scar.
auf bren - nen - der Fel - sen - wand.
its scorch - ing and rock - y scar.
auf bren - nen - der Fel - sen - wand.
its scorch - ing and rock - y scar.

27. So weich und warm

So soft and warm

Paul Heyse

PETER CORNELIUS
(1874)

6
cresc.
pp
- taut, als wenn ihr Aug' an dei - nem hängt, als wenn ihr
doch, dass dei - ner Mut - ter Kind du warst, dass dei - ner
you as when her eyes be - hold your face, as when her
- gain that you were born your mo - ther's child, that you were
cresc.
pp
- taut, als wenn ihr Aug' an dei - nem hängt, als wenn ihr
doch, dass dei - ner Mut - ter Kind du warst, dass dei - ner
you as when her eyes be - hold your face, as when her
- gain that you were born your mo - ther's child, that you were
cresc.
pp
dich ü - ber - taut, als wenn ihr Aug' an dei - nem hängt, ihr
be - glückt dich doch, dass dei - ner Mut - ter Kind du warst, der
en - ve - lopes you as when her eyes be - hold your face, her
give thanks a - gain that you were born your mo - ther's child, were
cresc.
pp
dich ü - ber - taut, als wenn ihr Aug' an dei - nem, ihr
be - glückt dich doch, dass dei - ner Mut - ter Kind, dei - ner
en - ve - lopes you as when her eyes be - hold, her
give thanks a - gain that you were born your mo - ther's, were
9
mf
Aug' an dei - nem hängt. Drum sei ge-sinnt
Mut - ter Kind du warst.
eyes be - hold your face. So now, my child,
born your mo - ther's child.
mf
Aug' an dei - nem hängt. Drum sei ge - sinnt als gu - tes
Mut - ter Kind du warst.
eyes be - hold your face. So now, my child, be good, be
born your mo - ther's child.
mf
Aug' an dei - nem hängt. Drum sei ge - sinnt als gu - tes
Mut - ter Kind du warst.
eyes be - hold your face. So now, my child, be good, be
born your mo - ther's child.
mf
Aug' an dei - nem hängt. Drum sei ge - sinnt als gu - tes
Mut - ter Kind du warst.
eyes be - hold your face. So now, my child, be good, be
born your mo - ther's child.

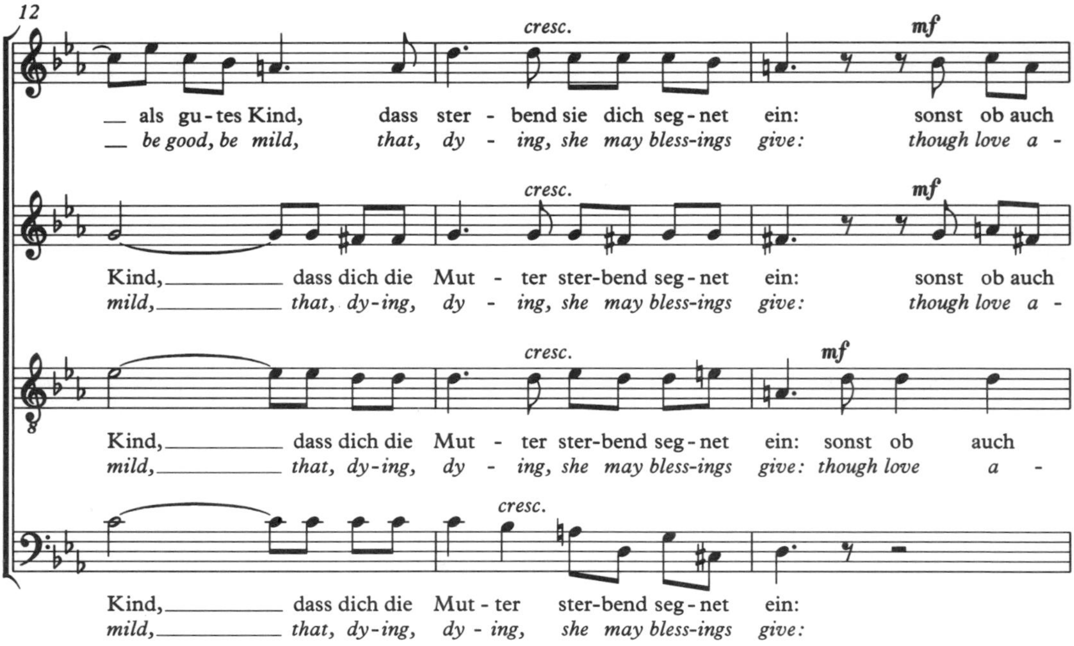
12
cresc.
mf
als gu-tes Kind, dass ster - bend sie dich seg-net ein: sonst ob auch
be good, be mild, that, dy - ing, she may bless-ings give: though love a -
Kind, dass dich die Mut - ter ster-bend seg-net ein: sonst ob auch
mild, that, dy-ing, dy - ing, she may bless-ings give: though love a -
Kind, dass dich die Mut - ter ster-bend seg-net ein: sonst ob auch
mild, that, dy-ing, dy - ing, she may bless-ings give: though love a -
Kind, dass dich die Mut-ter ster-bend seg-net ein:
mild, that, dy-ing, dy - ing, she may bless-ings give:

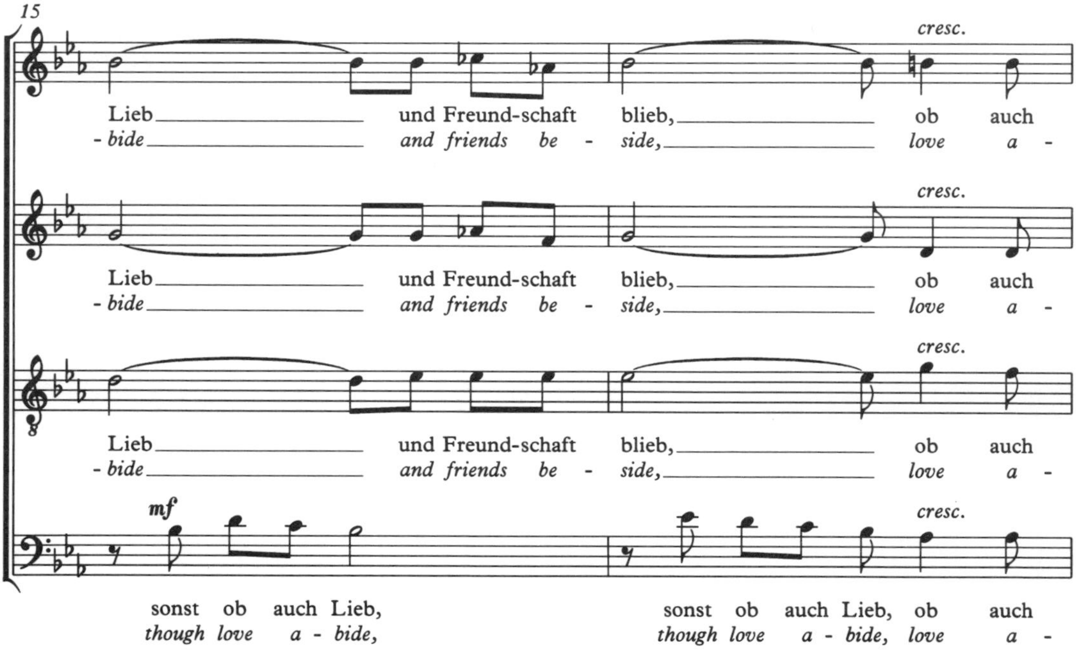
15
cresc.
mf
Lieb und Freund-schaft blieb, ob auch
-bide and friends be - side, love a -
Lieb und Freund-schaft blieb, ob auch
-bide and friends be - side, love a -
Lieb und Freund-schaft blieb, ob auch
-bide and friends be - side, love a -
sonst ob auch Lieb, sonst ob auch Lieb, ob auch
though love a - bide, though love a - bide, love a -

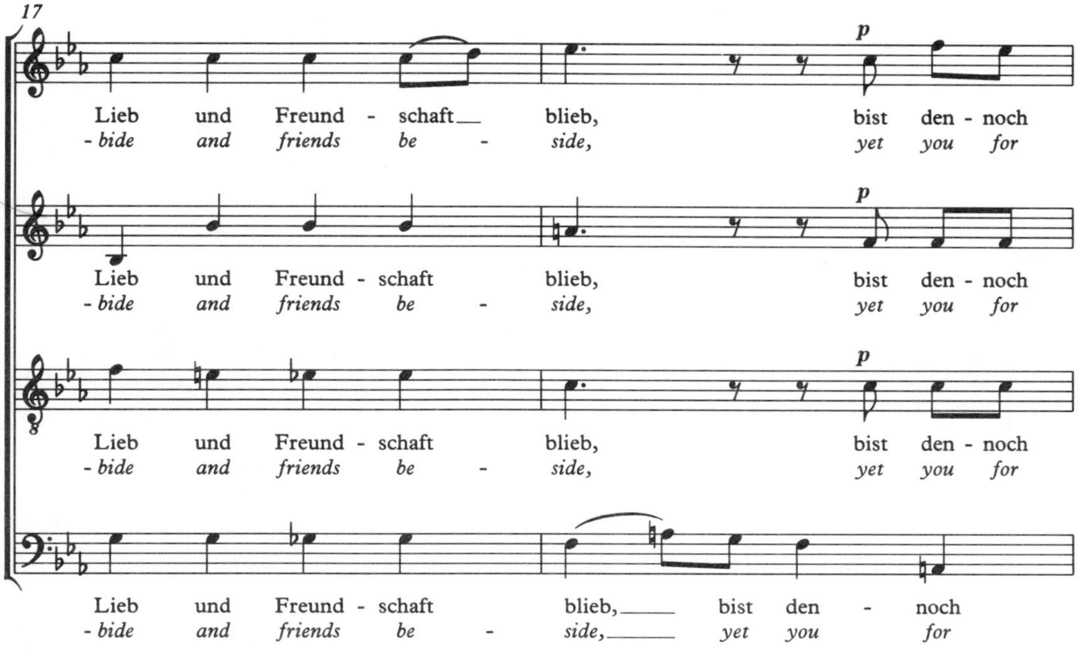
17
p
Lieb und Freund - schaft blieb, bist den - noch
- bide and friends be - side, yet you for
Lieb und Freund - schaft blieb, bist den - noch
- bide and friends be - side, yet you for
Lieb und Freund - schaft blieb, bist den - noch
- bide and friends be - side, yet you for
Lieb und Freund - schaft blieb, bist den - noch
- bide and friends be - side, yet you for

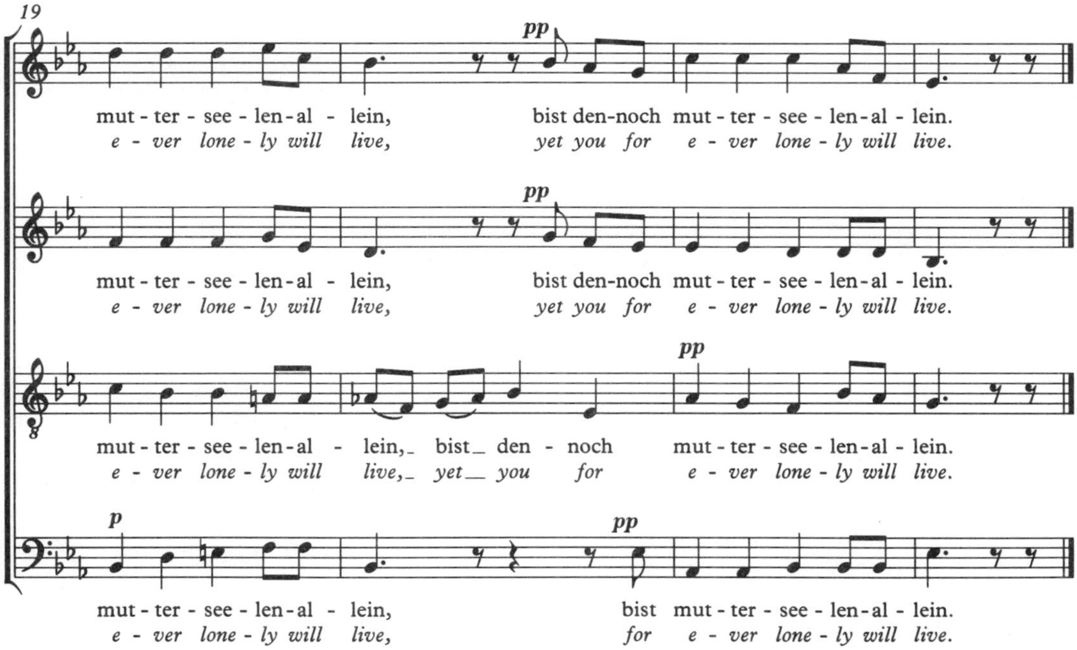
19
pp
mut - ter - see - len - al - lein, bist den-noch mut - ter - see - len - al - lein.
e - ver lone - ly will live, yet you for e - ver lone - ly will live.
mut - ter - see - len - al - lein, bist den-noch mut - ter - see - len - al - lein.
e - ver lone - ly will live, yet you for e - ver lone - ly will live.
mut - ter - see - len - al - lein, bist den - noch mut - ter - see - len - al - lein.
e - ver lone - ly will live, yet you for e - ver lone - ly will live.
p
mut - ter - see - len - al - lein, bist mut - ter - see - len - al - lein.
e - ver lone - ly will live, for e - ver lone - ly will live.

28. Du bist wie eine Blume

O you are like a flower

Heinrich Heine

ANTON BRUCKNER
(1861)

aufs
up -
12
mf
ist, mir ist als ob, als ob ich die Hän - de aufs Haupt, dir le - gen
long, I long to give, to give you a bless - ing, my hands up - on your
mf
dir
in
Haupt dir le - gen sollt,
- on your head in prayer,
16
be - tend, dass Gott dich er - hal - te, Gott
sollt, dir le - gen sollt, pray - ing that God may pre - serve you, God
head, your head in prayer,
le - gen sollt, be-tend, dass Gott dich er - hal - te,
prayer, in prayer, pray-ing that God may pre - serve you,
20
[p]
dich er - hal - te, be - tend, dass Gott dich er - hal - -
may pre - serve you, pray - ing that God may pre - serve
[p]
25
- te so rein, so rein und schön und hold, so schön, so rein und schön und hold.
you so fine, so fine and pure and fair, so pure, so fine and pure and fair.

29. Das edle Herz

The noble heart

Ernst Marinelli

ANTON BRUCKNER
(*c.*1862)

selbst ge - bo - ren
hu - man weak - ness
10
selbst___ ge - bo - ren son - dern sei - nem Schöp - fer___ glaubt,
hu - man weak - ness in___ his ma - ker yet___ be - lieves,___
sich___ selbst ge - bo - ren son - dern
know-ing hu-man weak - ness in his
13
die - sen Glau-ben nicht ver - lo - ren an - dern, an-dern sel - ben nie ge - raubt.
wor - ships God in faith and meek - ness, ne - ver,___ ne - ver o - ther___ men de - ceives.
17
mf
Wer den Werth der eig - nen___ Ha - be gern in dürft-ge Hän - de___ legt
He whose wealth makes him___ not___ greed - y glad - ly all his means im - parts,
mf
auch in frem - de, in frem - de
sha-ring love, sha-ring love with
21
p
[f]
f
sei - nes Wis-sens heh - re Ga - be auch in frem - de
in his wish to help the need - y sha-ring love with
f
f

24
Her - zen trägt, auch in___ frem - de Her - zen trägt. Wer im Seg - nen_
un - known hearts, sha - ring___ love with un-known hearts. He_ who takes his_
in frem - de
with un-known,
28
dem_ er - schal -
his__ the best,
und Be-glü-cken sei - nes Le - bens Freu - de_ weiss
great - est plea-sure gi - ving bless - ings_ kind - ly_ meant,
dem er -
his__ the
dem_ er - schal -
his__ the best,
dem er -
his__ the
32
- let mit Ent - zü - cken: dem_ er - schal-let mit Ent - zü - cken:
__ most va-lued trea - sure, his__ the best, most va-lued trea - sure:
- schal-let mit Ent - zü - cken, dem_ er-schal - - let mit Ent - zü - cken:
best, most va-lued treas - ure, his__ the best, most va-lued trea - sure:
- let mit Ent - zü - cken, dem_ er - schal-let mit Ent - zü - cken:
__ most va-lued trea - sure, his__ the best, most va-lued trea - sure:
- schal-let mit Ent - zü - cken, dem_ er-schal - let, er - schal-let mit Ent - zü - cken:
best, most va-lued trea - sure, his__ the best, his the best, most va-lued trea - sure:
35
langsam [slowly]
dank - er - füll - ter See - len - preis, dank - er - füll - ter__ See - len-preis.
his the soul with thanks con - tent, his___ the soul with_ thanks con-tent.

30. Wahlspruch
Motto

Karl Kerschbaum

ANTON BRUCKNER
(1868)

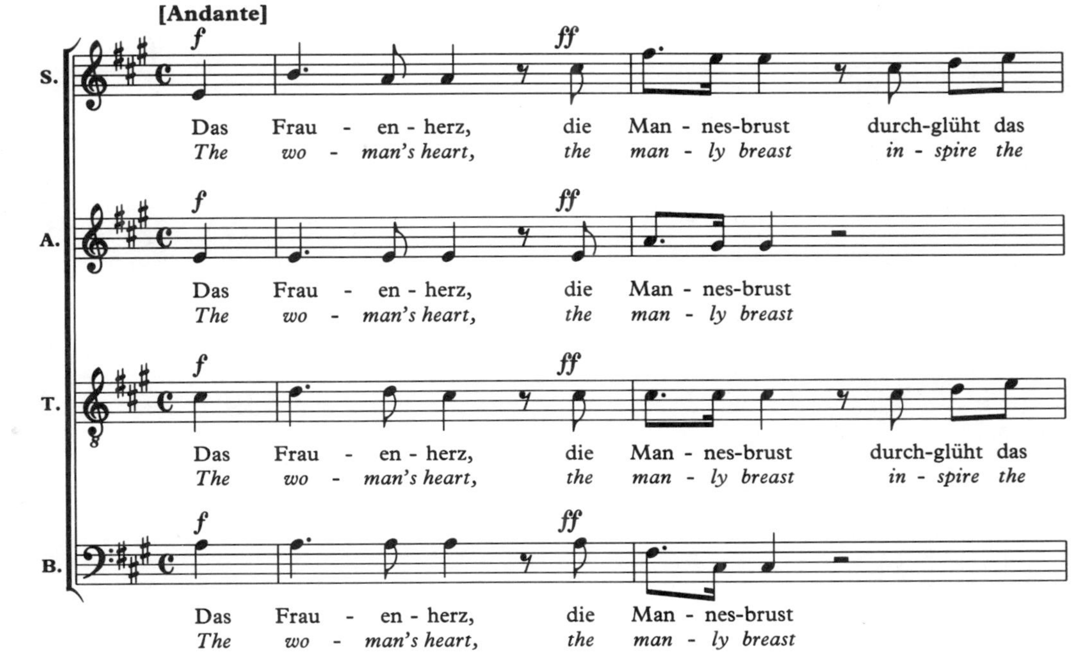

31. Dein Herzlein mild

Your gentle heart

Paul Heyse

JOHANNES BRAHMS
Op.62 no.4

8
p
kom - men, wird bald, wird bald zu Ta - ge
Hal - de, und duf - tet, und duf - tet durch die
- stow - ing, your heart, your heart with fire be -
mea - dow, their fra - grance, their fra - grance fills the
kom - men, wird bald, wird bald, wird bald zu Ta - ge
Hal - de, und duf - tet, und duf - tet, und duf - tet durch die
- stow - ing, your heart, your heart, your heart with fire be -
mea - dow, their fra - grance, their fra - grance, their fra-grance fills the
Ta - ge kom - men, wird bald, wird bald zu Ta - ge
durch die Hal - de, und duf - tet, duf - tet durch die
fire be - stow - ing, your heart, your heart with fire be -
fills the mea - dow, their fra - grance, fra-grance fills the
Ta - ge kom - men, wird bald zu Ta - ge, bald zu Ta - ge
durch die Hal - de, und duf - tet, und duf - tet durch die
fire be - stow - ing, your heart with fire, your heart with fire be -
fills the mea - dow, their fra - grance, their fra-grance fills the
11
[p]
kom-men.
Hal - de.
- stow - ing.
mea - dow.
3. Die Lie - be sacht hat ü - ber Nacht dir Tau ins Herz ge -
3. By eve-ning's end love's gen - tle hand with dew your heart has

poco f
15
S.
A.
- gos - sen, und Mor-gens dann, man sieht dirs an, das Knösp - lein ist er -
show-er'd, and when the dawn breaks in - to morn, the bud at last has
T.
B.
poco f
das Knösp - lein
the bud at
ist er - schlos -
last has flo -
p
19
- schlos - sen, das Knösp - lein, das Knösp - lein ist er - schlos - sen,
flo - wer'd, has flo - wer'd, the bud at last has flo - wer'd,
p
ist er - schlos - sen, das Knösp - lein
last has flo - wer'd, the bud at
- sen, ist er - schlos - sen, ist er - schlos-sen.
- wer'd, now has flo - wer'd, now has flo - wer'd.
22
mf
p
ist er-schlos - sen, das Knösp - lein ist er - schlos-sen.
now has flo - wer'd, the bud at last has flo - wer'd.
mf
p

32. Im Herbst

In autumn

Klaus Groth

JOHANNES BRAHMS
Op.104 no.5

9
p
dolce
- ab. Still ist die Flur, und nach_ dem Sü - den
ein. Früh kommt die Nacht: denn al - le Kräf - te
gloom. Si - lent the field, the birds_ drift south - wards,
day. Swift comes the night, all en - er - gies_ re -
- ab. Still ist die Flur, und nach dem Sü - den
ein. Früh kommt die Nacht: denn al - le Kräf - te
gloom. Si - lent the field, the birds drift south-wards,
day. Swift comes the night, all en - er - gies re -
- ab. Still ist die Flur, und nach dem Sü - den
ein. Früh kommt die Nacht: denn al - le Kräf - te
gloom. Si - lent the field, the birds drift south-wards,
day. Swift comes the night, all en - er - gies re -
- ab. Still ist die Flur,_ und nach dem Sü - den
ein. Früh kommt die Nacht: denn al - le Kräf - te
gloom. Si - lent the field,_ the birds_ drift south - wards,
day. Swift comes the night,_ all en - er - gies re -
13
p sempre
pp
wal - len die Sän - ger stumm, wie nach dem Grab, wie nach dem
fei - ern, und tief ver - schlos - sen ruht das Sein, ruht das
fly - ing yet hushed, as if to - wards the tomb, to - wards the
- lin - quish their pow'rs, and life is locked a - way, is locked a -
wal - len die Sän - ger stumm, wie nach_ dem_ Grab, wie nach dem
fei - ern, und tief ver - schlos - sen ruht_ das_ Sein, ruht das
fly - ing yet hushed, as if to - wards the_ tomb, to - wards the
- lin - quish their pow'rs, and life is locked a - way, is locked a -
wal - len die Sän - ger stumm, wie nach_ dem Grab, wie nach dem
fei - ern, und tief ver - schlos - sen ruht_ das Sein, ruht das
fly - ing yet hushed, as if to - wards_ the tomb, to - wards the
- lin - quish their pow'rs, and life is locked_ a - way, is locked a -
wal - len die Sän - ger stumm, wie nach dem Grab, wie nach dem
fei - ern, und tief_ ver - schlos - sen ruht das Sein, ruht das
fly - ing yet hushed, as if_ to - wards the tomb, to - wards the
- lin - quish their pow'rs, and life_ is locked a - way, is locked a -

19
[p] dolce
espress. cresc.
Grab. Sein. tomb. - way.
3. Sanft wird der Mensch. Er sieht die Son - ne sin - ken,
3. How frail is man. He sees the sun de - cli - ning,
3. Sanft wird der Mensch. Er sieht die Son - ne sin - ken, er
3. How frail is man. He sees the sun de - cli - ning, he
3. Sanft wird der Mensch. Er sieht die Son - ne sin - ken, er
3. How frail is man. He sees the sun de - cli - ning, he
3. Sanft wird der Mensch. Er sieht die Son - ne sin - ken,
3. How frail is man. He sees the sun de - cli - ning,
24
f
p
er ahnt, er ahnt des Le-bens wie des Jah - res
he dreads, he dreads life's out-come as the years pass
ahnt, er ahnt des Le - bens wie des Jah - res
dreads, he dreads life's out - come as the years pass
ahnt, er ahnt des Le - bens wie des Jah - res
dreads, he dreads life's out - come as the years pass
er ahnt, er ahnt des Le-bens wie des Jah - res
he dreads, he dreads life's out-come as the years pass

29
pp
cresc.
Schluss. Feucht wird das Aug, doch in der Trä - ne Blin - ken, doch
by. Eyes fill with tears, yet through the tear - drops shi - ning, yet
Schluss. Feucht wird das Aug, doch in der Trä - ne Blin - ken, doch
by. Eyes fill with tears, yet through the tear-drops shi - ning, yet
Schluss. Feucht wird das Aug, doch in der Trä - ne Blin - ken, doch
by. Eyes fill with tears, yet through the tear - drops shi - ning, yet
Schluss. Feucht wird das Aug, doch in der Trä - ne Blin - ken, doch
by. Eyes fill with tears, yet through the tear - drops shi - ning, yet
34
f
in der Trä - ne Blin - ken ent - strömt des Her - zens
through the tear - drops shi - ning pour forth most heart - felt
in der Trä - ne Blin - ken ent - strömt, ent - strömt des Her - zens
through the tear - drops shi - ning pour forth, pour forth most heart - felt
in der Trä - ne Blin - ken ent - strömt, ent - strömt des Her - zens
through the tear - drops shi - ning pour forth, pour forth most heart - felt
in der Trä - ne Blin - ken ent - strömt, ent - strömt des Her - zens
through the tear - drops shi - ning pour forth, pour forth most heart - felt
38
p dolce
dim.
pp
se - lig-ster Er - guss, se - lig - ster Er - guss.
words of bliss and joy, words of bliss and joy.
se - lig-ster Er - guss, se - lig - ster Er - guss.
words of bliss and joy, words of bliss and joy.
se - lig - ster Er - guss, se - lig - ster Er - guss.
words of bliss and joy, words of bliss and joy.
se - lig - ster Er - guss, se - lig - ster Er - guss.
words of bliss and joy, words of bliss and joy.

33. In stiller Nacht
At dead of night

Folksong

JOHANNES BRAHMS
(pub. 1864)

34. Erlaube mir
Permit me

Folksong

JOHANNES BRAHMS
Deutsche Volkslieder, no.17

35. Da unten im Tale
Below in the valley

Folksong

JOHANNES BRAHMS
Deutsche Volkslieder, no.19

2 Sprichst allweil von Liebe,
  sprichst allweil von Treu,
und a bissele Falschheit
  is au wol dabei.

3 Und wenn i dirs zehnmal sag,
  dass i di lieb,
und du willst nit verstehen,
  muss i halt weitergehn.

4 Für die Zeit, wo du g'liebt mi hast,
  dank i dir schön,
und i wünsch, dass dir anderswo
  besser mag gehn.

2 Your talk is of love
  and of constancy true,
and some lying and falsehood
  is always there too.

3 If I say 'I love you'
  yet ten times or more,
and you will not believe me,
  I cannot still endure.

4 For the time when you loved me,
  with thanks my heart melts,
and I hope you'll be better off
  with someone else.

36. Dem dunkeln Schoss der heilgen Erde

In earth's dark womb

Friedrich von Schiller

JOHANNES BRAHMS
(pre–1864)

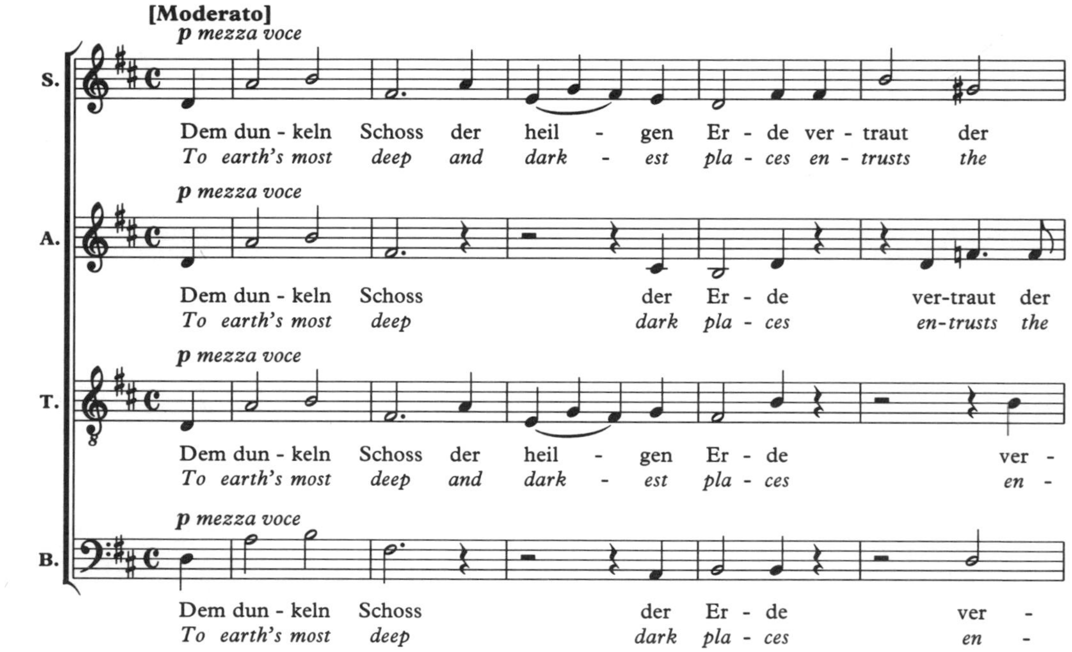

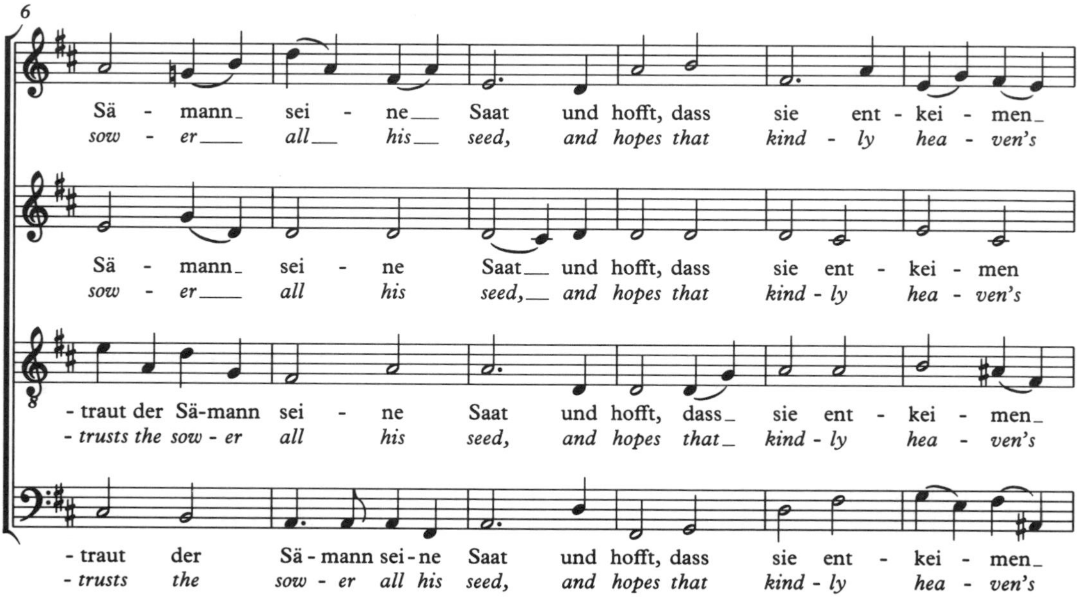

12
[p]
wer - de zum Se - gen nach des Him - mels Rat. Noch
gra - ces en - gen - der life, that crops may breed. More
wer - de zum Se - gen nach des Him - mels Rat.
gra - ces en - gen - der life, that crops may breed.
p
wer - de zum Se - gen nach des Him - mels Rat. Noch köst - li -
gra - ces en - gen - der life, that crops may breed. More pre - cious
wer - de zum Se - gen nach des Him - mels Rat.
gra - ces en - gen - der life, that crops may breed.
18
cresc.
köst - li - che - ren Sa - men, noch köst - li - che - ren
pre - cious seeds we bu - ry, more pre - cious seeds we
[p]
Noch köst - li - che - ren Sa -
More pre - cious seeds we bu -
- che - ren Sa - men, noch köst -
seeds we bu - ry, more pre -
Noch köst - li - che - ren, noch köst - li - che - ren
More pre - cious seeds, more pre - cious seeds we
23
Sa - men ber - gen wir trau - ernd, wir trau -
bu - ry, che - rish in mourn - ing, in mourn -
- men ber - gen wir trau - ernd, wir trau - ernd,
- ry, che - rish in mourn - ing, in mourn - ing,
- li - che-ren ber - gen wir trau - ernd, wir trau - ernd, wir
- cious seeds we che - rish in mourn - ing, in mourn - ing, in
Sa - men ber - gen wir trau - ernd, wir
bu - ry, che - rish in mourn - ing, in

28
f
p
[p]
-ernd, wir trau - ernd in der Er-de Schoss und
-ing, in mourn - ing, to the earth do-nate, and
wir trau - ernd in der Er-de, in der Er - de Schoss
in mourn - ing, to the earth, to the earth do-nate,
trau - ernd in der Er-de, in der Er - de Schoss und
mourn - ing, to the earth, to the earth do-nate, and
trau - ernd in der Er - de Schoss und
mourn - ing, to the earth do - nate, and
33
hof-fen, dass er aus den Sär-gen er-blü-hen soll zu
hope that from their graves they flou-rish to com-pre-hend the
und hof-fen, dass er aus den Sär-gen er-blü-hen soll zu
and hope that from their graves they flou-rish to com-pre-hend the
hof-fen, dass er aus den Sär-gen er-blü-hen soll zu
hope that from their graves they flou-rish to com-pre-hend the
hof-fen, dass er aus den Sär-gen er-blü-hen soll zu
hope that from their graves they flou-rish to com-pre-hend the
39
pp
schö-nerm, schö-nerm Los, zu schö-nerm Los.
no-blest, no-blest fate, the no-blest fate.
schö-nerm, schö-nerm Los, zu schö-nerm Los.
no-blest, no-blest fate, the no-blest fate.
schö-nerm, schö-nerm Los, zu schö-nerm Los.
no-blest, no-blest fate, the no-blest fate.
schö-nerm Los, zu schö-nerm, schö-nerm Los.
no-blest fate, the no-blest, no-blest fate.

37. Grablied
Song at the sepulchre

Lenz Lorenzi

HUGO WOLF
(1876)

*Semichorus

38. Fröhliche Fahrt
Pleasant journey

Edmund Hoefer

HUGO WOLF
Op.17 no.1

2 Hinaus, hinaus mit Sing und Sang,
hinein ins Blau, ins Blau!
Der Tag mit klarem Fittich sank
auf Wald und Busch und Au.
Was zaghaft dir das Herz umschlingt,
wirf's ab, du altes Haus,
und zieh' noch einmal lustbeschwingt
zur Ferne froh hinaus,
und zieh' noch einmal lustbeschwingt
zu der Ferne froh hinaus!

2 Away, away with tune and song,
the azure sky is free!
The day on pinions bright has gone
from meadow, bush and tree.
O now throw off all dreary things,
the dolour and decay,
and once again on joyful wings
to distant love away,
and once again on joyful wings
to your distant love away!

39. Gottvertrauen
Confidence in God

August Mahlmann

HUGO WOLF
(*c.*1876)

2 Durch Wolken bricht der Hoffnung Licht
zur Erdenwelt herab;
wer's aufnahm in sein frommes Herz,
der wandelt ohne Furcht und Schmerz
mit Gottvertraun zum stillen Grab!

2 *Through clouds there shines on all mankind*
hope's radiance from above;
to those whose hearts will hope retain,
freedom is theirs from fear and pain,
in God they trust beyond the grave.

40. Ei, du Lütte

O, you little one

Klaus Groth

Arnold Schoenberg
(*c.* 1895–8)

23
all wat smuck is, och, ik seeg dat all dar - in! Funn ik blot dar - in, du Lüt - te,
all that's grace-ful, all is there by your de - sign! Could I find in them the best thing,
29
rit.
[a tempo]
ok dat Be - ste: du weerst min! Ei, du Lüt-te, Sö - te,
then, my sweet one, you'd be mine! O, you lit - tle sweet one,
34
Wit - te, ei, du Lüt - te, weerst du min! Wull di ple-gen, wull di
pure one, would that you could be but mine! I would love you, I would
39
Breit [Broadly]
molto rit.
he - gen, schust min Schatz, min De-mant sin, Schust min Schatz, min De - mant sin!
hold you, be my trea - sure, dia-mond fine, be my trea - sure, dia - mond fine!

Editorial Notes

Editorial Method

No transpositions or alterations to key-signatures, time-signatures, or note-values have been undertaken. C clefs in the sources have been replaced where necessary with the modern combination of clefs for SATB. Accidentals, including cautionary ones, are generally as given in the sources unless otherwise indicated. Dynamics are as given in the sources, editorially extended where appropriate to apply to all voice-parts. Tempo markings are as given in the sources, translations of those in German are supplied editorially. Other material editorially added, such as editorial accidentals and suggested tempo markings where these are absent from the sources, is shown in square brackets.

Archaic spellings (for example 'Thurm') have been editorially modernized. ß is replaced by ss. Capitalization, spelling, and punctuation have been made consistent among all voice-parts. Text-underlay is as given in the sources; however, where underlay in one voice-part is clearly intended to provide the model for voice-parts lacking text, the missing underlay has been editorially completed without comment. The editorial notes that follow are selective, and do not provide information that is readily available from other sources.

All English translations are editorial: the prose summary translations, being free from the constraints of the music, reflect the meanings of the German poems more closely than is usually possible in the case of translations for singing. The prose translations are intended as guidance for English-speaking performers who prefer to sing the German texts but would welcome translations, possibly for use as the basis of programme notes.

Editorial Notes

FRANZ SCHUBERT

2. Das Grab (The grave)

D643a, composed 1819, published 1972. ed. A. Weinmann (Vienna, 1972). From a manuscript discovered in 1971 in the music archive of Seitenstetten Abbey, Lower Austria. See A. Weinmann 'Zwei neue Schubertfunde' *Österreichische Musikzeitschrift*, xxvii (1972), pp. 75–78.

ROBERT SCHUMANN

12. John Anderson

Op. 67 no. 5, composed and published 1849. Schumann set this text for SATB again soon afterwards: the second setting is op. 145 no. 4. English texts for the present edition are taken from ed. J. Kinsley *Robert Burns: Poems and Songs* (London, 1969) p. 419. The English singing version reflects Burns's original text as far as the music allows. Burns's original spelling has not been retained in the edition, but is given with the prose translations.

13. Der Rekrut (The recruit)

Op. 75 no. 4, composed 1849, published 1850. English texts for the present edition are taken from ed. J. Kinsley *Robert Burns: Poems and Songs* (London, 1969) pp. 477–8. The English singing version reflects Burns's original text as far as the music allows. Burns's original spelling has not been retained in the edition, but is given with the prose translations. See the latter also for details of the apparently spurious third text verse.

PETER CORNELIUS

All pieces except 'So weich und warm': autograph manuscripts in Vienna, Österreichische Nationalbibliothek, Musiksammlung, previously unpublished. Catalogue details in G. Wagner *Peter Cornelius: Verzeichnis seiner musikalischen und literarischen Werke* (Tutzing, 1986) pp. 33–43.

21. Der Traum (The dream)

Mus. Hs. 4757, ff. 1r–2v. Composed 1842. The source is the composer's revised sketch in which there are numerous alterations. Possible errors which have evidently been allowed by the composer to stand, such as consecutive fifths by contrary motion at bars 23–24, TB, have been retained in the edition. The crotchet rest concluding all parts in the source has been omitted to accommodate the opening anacrusis.

22. Nichts ohne Liebe (Nothing without love)

Mus. Hs. 4752 ff. 16r–16v. Composed 1842. The source is the composer's revised sketch in which there are numerous alterations. Only the first text verse is underlaid: the remaining three are written out at the ends of the pages where space remains after the music.

23. Die Sternlein (The little stars)

Mus. Hs. 4753 ff. 1r–2r. Composed 1842. This sketch bears occasional alterations. Possible errors which have evidently been allowed by the composer to stand, such as consecutive octaves in bar 1, ST, and bars 1–2, SB, have been retained in the edition. Bar 5, S: notes to 'sprachen: Wir' in the source are d'sharp, e', f'sharp. Only the first text verse is underlaid: the remaining two are written out on a separate page after the music.

24. Aetherische Geisterstimmen (Ethereal spirit-voices)

Mus. Hs. 4752 ff. 13r–14r. Composed probably 1842. The author of the text is unknown; it is unlikely to have been Cornelius himself. The source is the composer's revised sketch in which alterations are very numerous. The many instances of possible error which have evidently been allowed by the composer to stand have been retained in the edition. The layout of the piece, the nature of the bass part and the occasional occurrence of figuring under this part suggest that this music may have been originally intended as part of a larger piece, probably with instrumental accompaniment. Bar 39, S: the word 'Violinschlüssel' (treble clef) is written above the stave; the music reverts to the C clef at bar 43. The note pitches in the edition have been altered accordingly. Bar 49, T: first note is f' in the source. The crotchet rest concluding all parts in the source has been omitted to accommodate the opening anacrusis.

25. Frühlingsglaube (Belief in springtime)
Mus. Hs. 4752 ff. 17^{r-v}. Composed 1842. An autograph of the same piece for male voices is also extant and it is not clear which was the first version to be composed, although Cornelius records having sung the male-voice version with three friends in winter 1843. The tempo marking, absent in the version for mixed voices, is taken from the male-voice version. The source is the composer's revised sketch in which only the first verse is underlaid, the second being written out on spare staves after the music. The minim followed by crotchet in the final bar in all parts has been altered to accommodate the opening anacrusis.

26. Der Fichtenbaum (The fir-tree)
Mus. Hs. 4755 ff. 2r–2v. Composed probably 1842. This autograph was possibly intended as a fair copy. Bar 36, SB: the consecutive octaves occur in the source and are retained. The crotchet rest concluding all parts in the source has been omitted to accommodate the opening anacrusis.

ANTON BRUCKNER

28. Du bist wie eine Blume (O you are like a flower)
Composed 1861, apparently unpublished. Manuscript sketches in Vienna, Österreichische Nationalbibliothek, Musiksammlung S. m. 3166. Manuscript sketches reproduced in facsimile in ed. A. Göllerich and M. Auer *Anton Bruckner: ein Lebens- und Schaffensbild* (Regensburg, 1922–37) vol. iii part 2. The sketches are very heavily altered. Bars 17–21: two slightly different completed versions of this passage are extant in the source as well as a partly-completed but deleted sketch. The present edition reproduces what seems to have been Bruckner's final working of this passage.

29. Das edle Herz (The noble heart)
Composed c.1862. Three versions in manuscript in Vienna, Österreichische Nationalbibliothek, Musiksammlung S. m. 19.780, 19.751, 19.752; ed. A. Göllerich and M. Auer *Op. cit.*

30. Wahlspruch (Motto)
Composed 1868. ed. A. Göllerich and M. Auer *Op. cit.*

English Prose Texts

1. Chor der Engel (Angels' Chorus)
Christ is risen! Joy to mortal man, afflicted by pernicious, lingering, hereditary shortcomings.

2. Das Grab (The grave)
1. The grave is deep and motionless, and its edge terrible; it covers an unknown land with a black veil. 2. The nightingales' song does not sound in its depth; the roses of friendship merely fall on to the moss on the mound. 3. Forsaken brides wring their sore hands in vain; the laments of orphans do not penetrate the depth of the ground. 4. But nowhere else is longed-for peace to be found; only through the gloomy portal can one enter one's homeland. 5. On earth the poor heart is buffeted by many a storm; only where it no longer beats can it attain true peace.

3. Des Menschen Trost (Mankind's solace)
1. To him in whom righteous memories flourish, transitoriness is affliction; the heart that always glows with love, in dreams can summon a golden age! And if night engulfs it when it is tossed about by life's tempests, a deep longing wells up in mankind, hope is his solace!
2. And when spring, with its joy, is about to leave us in autumn, the soul is aware that nothing on earth can last forever. And when the splendour of May has gone and the sweet memory of a lovely time has faded, a deep longing wells up in mankind, hope is his solace! 3. To him in whom righteous memories flourish, transitoriness is affliction. The heart wearied by hatred is ever so far from its goal; and then, when it finally awakens, deceived, at the graveside in winter's cold, a deep longing wells up in mankind, hope is his solace!

4. Im Vorübergehn (In passing by)
I was strolling over the fields, seeking nothing, that was my intention. All at once there stood a little flower so close to me that in all my life I had seen nothing more lovely. I wanted to pick it, but hurriedly it said: 'I have roots that are hidden deep down, I am established in the deep soil; that is why my blossoms are so beautifully shaped. I cannot flirt, I cannot creep, you must not pick me, you must transplant me.' I was strolling through the woods; I was so happy I wanted to go on and on, that was my intention.

5. In der Marienkirche (In the church of the Virgin Mary)
They buried him in the church of the Virgin Mary and her they buried in its chancel; a little red rose sprouted from her grave, from his a hawthorn came forth. They grew towards each other, their branches began to entwine as if they liked to be close to each other, so that everyone could see that two lovers were at rest there.

6. Morgengebet (Morning prayer)
1. O wonderful deep silence, how solitary it still is in the world. The woodlands gently bow, as though the Lord passed through the quiet fields. 2. I feel as if I were born anew; where now is anxiety and distress? As the sun rises I feel ashamed of the things that used to make me weary. 3. The world with its sorrow and happiness I will, as a pilgrim, gladly enter; merely as a bridge to you, Lord, across the river of time.

7. Herbstlied (Autumn song)
Lovely spring, you have gone! Nowhere may you stay! Autumn's uneasy forces bluster where once I saw your joyful blossoms. How mournfully the wind sweeps through the bush, as if it were weeping. Sighs of dying nature shiver through the withered woodland. O how soon once again a year has slipped away from me! It rushes through the wood, demanding 'Has your heart found happiness?'. Forest murmurs, how wonderfully you have touched my heart! Indeed, every year brings new foliage and new hope alike.

8. Frühzeitiger Frühling (Early springtime)
1. Days of rapture, do you come so soon, giving me sunshine, hill and woodland? The stream flows more fully, and can these be the meadows, can that be the valley? 2. Blue-tinted freshness! Heaven and height! Golden fishes teeming in the lake. Gaily-coloured plumage fluttering in the woodland; heavenly songs sounding within it. Beneath the vigour of the verdant blossoms the buzzing bees sample the nectar. A gentle stirring trembles in the breeze; enchanting movement, heady fragrance. Soon a livelier breeze stirs, losing itself immediately among the bushes. But it returns to my heart. Muses, help me to bear my happiness! Tell me, what has happened to me since yesterday? Lovely sisters, my sweetheart is here!

9. Abschied vom Wald (Farewell to the forest)
1. O distant vales, O heights, O beautiful green forest, you are my pleasure and sorrow, devoted place of rest! Out there, constantly deluded, the busy world hurtles by. Green canopy, wrap yourself around me once again. 2. A silent, serious word is written in the forest about righteousness, love, and the ideals of mankind. I have faithfully read these simple, sincere words, and they became incontrovertibly clear to my entire being. 3. Soon I shall leave you, to go as a stranger into unknown regions, to see life's drama among teeming alleyways. And in the midst of life the power of your integrity will exalt me in my loneliness, so that my heart will never grow old.

10. Ruhetal (Valley of rest)
When golden mountains of cloud gather in the final rays of daylight, looking like the Alps, often then I tearfully ask myself: is my longed-for valley of rest perhaps to be found there?

11. Jägerlied (Huntsman's song)
How dainty the bird's footstep is in the snow, when it traverses the mountain top. How much more daintily my beloved's dear hand writes, when she writes a note to me

in a distant country. High into the air ascends a heron, whence neither arrow nor shot can fly: thoughts of true love can fly a thousand times as high and as swiftly!

12. John Anderson

1. John Anderson my jo [sweetheart], John,/when we were first acquent;/your locks were like the raven./Your bony brow was brent [smooth];/But now your brow is beld [bald], John,/Your locks are like the snaw;/But blessings on your frosty pow [head],/John Anderson my jo. 2. John Anderson my jo, John,/we clamb the hill the gither;/And mony a canty [lively, cheerful] day, John,/ We've had wi' ane anither:/Now we maun totter down, John,/And hand in hand we'll go;/And sleep the gither at the foot,/John Anderson my jo.

13. Der Rekrut (The recruit)

When first my brave Johnie lad came to this town,/He had a blue bonnet that wanted the crown,/But now he has gotten a hat and a feather,/Hey, brave Johnie lad, cock up your beaver [beaver hat]./Cock up your beaver, and cock it fu' [full, very] sprush [sprucely, smartly];/We'll over the border and gie them a brush;/There's somebody there we'll teach better behaviour,/Hey, brave Johnie lad, cock up your beaver.

The third verse of Schumann's partsong apparently does not originate from poetry by Robert Burns: If the bullets are whistling around your face, then think of your beloved and don't be afraid. And if you come back with a cut across your cheek: hooray, brave Johnnie, I will love you all the more!

14. Der Schmidt (The Blacksmith)

I can hear my sweetheart. He wields the hammer; it booms, it rings, it penetrates into the distance like a peal of bells through alleys and squares. At the black furnace, there stands my beloved, but I pass by; then the bellows hiss, the flames roar and blaze around him.

15. Sommerlied (Summer song)

1. The linden tree fashioned its dream, it was barely spring, yet the wind blew hard. Look how the dream of blossoms has blown away! 2. Feel how cold the breeze blows, see how the shrub remains withered which used to be so young. 3. The heart beats without joy and the breast bears pain. Once they rose, free and happy. 4. When you loved me, how clearly I saw in my mind's eye the joys of spring! 5. When I saw you depart, leaving me lonely: O how did I bear it, bereft of my life! May, where is your garland? Does no brightness attend you when love's sunshine melts away? Nightingale, launch yourself loudly into sound, lead me away to the rose in the grave, down into the grave.

16. Es ist ein Schnee gefallen (A fall of snow)

There has been a fall of snow even though it is not yet time; I cannot journey far, my path is covered with snow. My house has no gable, it has become old, the bolts seem to be shattered, my little room feels cold. Ah, love, take pity on me, for I am so miserable, and enfold me in your arms so that winter will depart.

17. Ave Maria

Ave Maria! Ocean and heaven are at rest. The chime of bells sounds from every tower. Ave Maria! Desist from earthly doings, O pray to the Virgin, pray to the Virgin's Son; Now the heavenly hosts themselves kneel, with wands of lilies, before the Father's throne, and through the rosy clouds the solemn songs of the blessed spirits waft below. O holy devotion, which wonderfully permeates every heart with gentle thrills, O holy faith, which soars heavenwards on the white wings of prayer! Pain is washed away in gentle tears, while the jubilation of happiness softly sounds. Ave Maria! When the bell rings, then earth and heaven are reconciled.

18. Er ist's! ('Tis he!)

Once again spring lets its blue riband flutter through the air, sweet familiar breezes waft the land with anticipation, violets are already dreaming, they want to blossom soon. Hark! the gentle note of a harp sounds in the distance! Spring, it's you! I sensed your presence!

19. Ritter Frühling (Spring, the handsome knight)

1. Spring is a strong hero, a knight without equal, his crest and badge are the red rose in the green field. He wielded his sword of sunshine boldly and tirelessly until the silver armour which winter had fashioned for himself burst into brightness. 2. And now he travels through billows and dry land with a triumphant call. The nightingale flies forth, preceding him as his herald. And all around, his call challenges every heart in every place, and even if it is encased in triple bronze it must open its portals to him. However tightly closed the portals it can never be exempt, and he must pay homage to love, his queen, whose champion he is.

20. Die Wasserrose (The water-lily)

The silent water-lily emerges from the blue lake, its leaves glimmer and flash, its chalice is as white as snow. From heaven the moon gives out its golden light, pouring forth all its rays into the flower's heart. In the water a white swan circles around the flower, singing so sweetly and softly, looking at the flower. It sings so sweetly, so softly, in singing it would die. O flower, white flower, can you understand the song?

21. Der Traum (The dream)

In the most beautiful garden two lovers wandered hand in hand. Two pale, ailing figures, they sat in the flowers' land. They kissed on the cheeks, they kissed on the mouth, they held each other tight, they grew young and well. Two bells sounded brightly, by and by the dream vanished. She lay in the convent's cell, he far away in the tower's ground.

22. Nichts ohne Liebe (Nothing without love)

1. Bird without peace or rest beats the lively wings, ever hops from branch to branch, but without love never, never! 2. Flower nods to flower, whispering in the morning's glimmer. Life, how beautiful you are! But without love never, never! 3. Waves exchange word for word, rippling along in silver sparkle. Gaily they move in twosomes, but without love never, never! 4. Man's heart full of joy and pain: do you not feel that you alone are for ever blest? But without love never, never!

23. Die Sternlein (The little stars)

1. And the sun, she journeyed on her fiery ride around the world. And the stars, they said 'We are travelling with you around the world'. But the sun, she chided them: 'You are staying at home, since I shall scorch your golden eyes on my fiery ride around the world.' 2. And the stars, they went to the lovely moon in the night. And they said 'You who are enthroned on the clouds in the night, let us travel with you, since your gentle light will never

scorch our eyes.' And he received them, companions of the night. 3. Now welcome, you stars, and you, good moon, in the night. You comprehend what quietly dwells in the heart in the night. Come and kindle the heavenly lights, that I may revel and join with you in the friendly games of the night.

24. Aetherische Geisterstimmen (Ethereal spirit-voices)
Ethereal ghostly voices, the larks' heavenly greetings, how sweetly your glorious voices stir my breast. I softly close my eyes and memories float by like evening twilight, fanned by a spring breeze.

25. Frühlingsglaube (Belief in springtime)
1. The gentle breezes have awakened, they waft and whisper day and night, and accomplish all that is needed. O refreshing fragrance, O new sound! Now, poor heart, do not be uneasy! Now everything, all must change. 2. Every day the world becomes more beautiful, one can never tell what might happen next! There seems to be no end to the blossom. The deepest, most remote valley bursts into bloom! Now, poor heart, forget your torment, now everything, all must change.

26. Der Fichtenbaum (The fir-tree)
A fir-tree stands lonely on the bare northern height. It is drowsy, with a white cover, wrapped round by ice and snow. It dreams of a palm tree which, far in the East, lonely and silently mourns on a fiery rocky wall.

27. So weich und warm (So soft and warm)
1. No arm cherishes you as softly and warmly as your mother's embrace. No comfort envelopes you as cosily as when her eyes gaze into yours. So be sure to be a good child so that at her death she blesses you: for although love and friendship endure, you will nevertheless be utterly alone. 2. And when you reach old age, faithfully retaining many a youthful memory, above all be happy that you were your mother's child: for although . . .

28. Du bist wie eine Blume (O you are like a flower)
You are just like a flower, so gracious, fair, and pure; I look at you and sadness steals into my heart. It is as if I should lay my hands upon your head, praying that God may keep you so pure and fair and gracious.

29. Das edle Herz (The noble heart)
1. Whoever does not cherish the flame of only his own altar in his bosom, whoever gladly turns a glance of selfless love towards his brother. 2. Whoever does not think he was born for himself but for his Creator's purpose, who has not lost this belief nor deprived others of it. 3. Whoever willingly puts the value of his possessions into needy hands, and imparts the noble gift of his knowledge to other hearts. 4. Whoever derives his life's pleasure from bestowing blessings and happiness, to him will accrue the exaltation of the praise of grateful souls.

30. Wahlspruch (Motto)
The woman's heart, the man's breast inspire the song with equal delight.

31. Dein Herzlein mild (Your gentle heart)
1. Your gentle heart, beloved image, is not yet set aglow, and soon will come the day when rapturous ardour will stir within it. 2. The night has brought dew to all the buds in the forest, and when morning comes they break into bloom and their fragrance wafts over the hillside. 3. Gently love has poured dew into your heart overnight, and when morning comes one can see that the little bud has opened.

32. Im Herbst (In autumn)
1. Autumn is sad. And when the leaves fall, so also sinks the heart into gloomy melancholy. How still the meadow is, and silently the singers journey southwards, as though towards the grave. 2. The day is wan, and pallid mists envelope the sun just as they shroud the heart. How early the night comes: all powers come to rest, and all existence is deeply locked away. 3. Man has grown mellow. He sees the sun setting, he has forebodings about life's and the year's ending. His eye becomes moist, but amid the glistening of tears the heart's most blissful effusions stream forth.

33. In stiller Nacht (At dead of night)
1. At dead of night, at first watch, a voice began to lament. The night wind sweetly and gently carried the sound to me. My heart is dissolved in bitter sorrow and sadness, I have watered all the little flowers with pure tears. 2. The lovely moon wants to set, for sorrow it no longer wishes to shine. The stars have put aside their glimmer, they want to weep with me. There is no birdsong nor joyful sound to be heard in the breeze. The wild animals, too, mourn with me among the rocks and ravines.

34. Erlaube mir (Permit me)
1. Fair maiden, permit me to go into the garden to see how beautiful the roses are. Permit me to pick them, it is high time. Their beauty, their promise has gladdened my heart. 2. O maiden, O maiden, you lonely child, who has put the idea into your heart that I ought not to see the garden and the roses? You delight my eyes, to that I must confess.

35. Da unten im Tale (Below in the valley)
1. In the valley below there runs muddy water, and I can't tell you how much I love you. 2. Constantly you speak of love and faithfulness, and there's a bit of falsehood there as well. 3. And if I tell you ten times over that I love you, and you won't understand, I'll just have to move on. 4. I thank you sincerely for the time when you loved me, and I hope you'll have better luck somewhere else.

36. Dem dunkeln Schoss der heilgen Erde (In earth's dark womb)
The sower entrusts his seed to the dark womb of the hallowed earth, and hopes that it will germinate with the blessing of heaven's decree. Mourning, we conceal even more valuable seeds in earth's womb, and hope that they will rise from their coffins to a more noble destiny.

37. Grablied (Song at the sepulchre)
Wake up! Awake again, smile at us once more—but no, slumber softly, weary one, having only just escaped from earth's folly. Slumber sweetly in eternal peace. May angels keep watch over you. May you, whom good fortune has shunned, find silent repose in the darkness of the grave.

38. Fröhliche Fahrt (Pleasant journey)
1. Lucky he who is on his way to his sweetheart in the far-off distance! His gait is dancelike, his song is merry, the sunshine sparkles. There is no word, no song that can describe the utter bliss so pure: lucky he who is on his way to his sweetheart in the far-off distance! 2. Away with song and singing, into the distant blue! The day, on wing, has gone down over wood, bush, and meadow. Old

friend, cast off what timorously clings to your heart, and once again be joyfully on your way into the distance!

39. Gottvertrauen (Confidence in God)

1. In heaven's height the stars move in their constant, silent path. Man, frail child of time, glimpses eternal splendour on high with absolute trust. 2. The light of hope shines down through clouds to the mortal world. He who receives it into his pious heart walks without fear and pain, with confidence in God to the silent grave.

40. Ei, du Lütte (O, you little one)

O, you little one, sweet one, pure one, O, you little one, were you but mine! I want to cherish you, want to look after you; you should be my treasure, my diamond! Ah, I look through your eyes, right into your quiet heart. Whether it can not be, little one, pure one, whether it can not be, that you were mine! All that is beautiful, all that is graceful; ah, I see all of that within. If only I could find the best thing, you little one, you would be mine!